TRAINING WITH POWER METERS

LOUIS PASSFIELD

FOREWORD BY ROB HAYLES

THE CROWOOD PRESS

D0910609

First published in 2015 by
The Crowood Press Ltd
Ramsbury, Marlborough
Wiltshire SN8 2HR

www.crowood.com

British Library Cataloguing-in-Publication Data
A catalogue record for this book is available from the British Library.

ISBN 978 1 84797 897 4

Frontispiece: Radu Razvan/Shutterstock.com

Typeset by Servis Filmsetting Ltd, Stockport, Cheshire

Printed and bound in Singapore by Craft Print International

TRAINING WITH POWER METERS

CONTENTS

FOREWORD
BY ROB HAYLES

Science in cycling has been there from the start of my career. Initially it was quite basic, before first advancing to using heart rate monitors in training and then, a little later on, to power-measuring cranks. Thanks to Louis, I was the first rider in the UK to use the German SRM power meter in a race. During the race, riders were coming up to me and joking, 'What's on ITV?' or 'Can you get Eurosport on that?' But in recent years power meters have come on in leaps and bounds. With modern power meters and help from guys like Louis and the other team physiologists, I was able to implement my training much better than was previously the case.

In recent years, especially within the last decade, other previously strong cycling nations, Italy and Germany for instance, which led the way, are now looking at Britain and seeing what we do. From a British point of view cycling has turned itself on its head. One of the major factors in British Cycling's success has been its strong coaching and scientific input and the use of power meters has been central to this. Louis was the first person I knew to start working with a power meter. In this book he uses this scientific and coaching experience to explain clearly and simply how to get the best out of yourself by training with a power meter.

Rob Hayles is a successful former professional cyclist who now presents regularly on television. On the track, Rob won two World titles and three Olympic medals. He was a member of the British Cycling team for more than sixteen years with team mates Sir Bradley Wiggins and Mark Cavendish.

Rob Hayles competing in the Tour of Britain.

PREFACE

When I was younger I wanted to win the Tour de France. It was the reason I studied sports science at university and learnt about the science of training. I tried to apply this knowledge to my own bike training and became a successful cyclist.

Shortly after graduating I made it to an Olympic training camp. At dinner I sat at the same table as Sir Steve Redgrave. Even before the 1992 Olympics, with many years still to row before his fifth gold medal, he was already a sporting legend. I was there with other dedicated athletes preparing for the 1992 Barcelona Olympics. It was a heady experience. To get there I had spent a decade dedicated to bike training and extending myself further with academic study. This was why on the last day of the

camp I was sat in the team car alongside the national coach, reflecting on how things had worked out for me. I was watching several members of the Great Britain team dominate a road race. The only thing was that these were younger, junior raw talents powering away on their bikes. And with all my physical and academic training I realized that I could perform better as a scientist than as a cyclist.

A quarter of a century later I continue to study and research training. I have witnessed first hand exciting developments in cycling and training. I can even claim to have added a little to what is understood about the science of training. And along the way I have had the privilege of working with some of the best riders and coaches in the world.

This book is about sharing some of the benefits of this experience. You do not have to be a serious competitive cyclist, triathlete or coach to read this book. You just have to be interested in improving fitness and be motivated to find ways of doing it more effectively, especially on a bike and by training with a power meter. I hope you find it useful.

2014 Tour winner Vincenzo Nibali, during Stage 14, Col du Lautaret. (Radu Razvan/ Shutterstock.com)

INTRODUCTION

In July 1992 Chris Boardman won Great Britain's first track cycling gold medal for seventy-two years on the Barcelona Olympic velodrome. As he raced, I became clearer on what is required to reach the top step of the podium in one of the world's major cycling events. I was then British Cycling's sports scientist, working with Peter Keen, Boardman's mentor. I had returned to the UK from our Olympic training camp in Majorca just in time to watch the race on television. At home in Sussex, the BBC coverage allowed me to watch Boardman fly around the track on his black Lotus bike to catch his tall German rival, Jens Lehman. Having been the scientist for the Barcelona Olympic team I knew better than most what it had taken for Chris to succeed in his gold medal quest. In my flat, mounted on my own bike was an SRM power meter, probably the first to be seen in the UK. How I wished that we'd been able to install it on that Lotus before the Barcelona Olympic Games began. From laboratory testing we knew that Chris was in the form of his life. But we could still only guess at how he had performed during the race itself to set a new World and Olympic record.

Any data on elite athletes was extremely scarce in those days, and there were virtually no measurements available from actual competition. This was why I had been working on a special project earlier in the year, before the Olympic Games started. My aim was to better understand the demands of road racing and how hard the riders had to work during a stage race in particular. A heart rate monitor without wires that could record data was still quite novel in 1992. Polar had produced one and were keen for me to use it with the British team riding the Milk Race (a forerunner of the Tour of Britain). Using the Polar Sports Tester I was able to conduct ground-breaking research by recording the riders' heart rate each day of the stage race. From the riders' heart rate I could calculate their power output in order to estimate how hard they had worked. The problem with this approach is that your heart rate is not only affected by how hard you have worked. Lots of other factors – like excitement, tiredness, hydration and temperature – can affect your heart rate too. Of course these factors are part and parcel of stage racing. My calculations could therefore only ever be considered a crude approximation, no matter how cutting-edge the Polar heart rate monitor.

It was not until the following year (1993, the year after Boardman's Olympic success) that I was able to measure more precisely what it takes to be an elite road racer. I managed to persuade a promising local young rider to endure a battery of laboratory fitness tests and to let me fit a power meter to his bike. The national coach and I then followed the race anxiously in the GB cycling team car, hoping the young rider could last the pace. This is how Rob Hayles, later to become a double world champion, became the first to ride a premier UK road race with a power meter (much to the amusement of his rivals at the time, it has to be said). Later that year on the velodrome in Bordeaux, just as Miguel Indurain led the Tour de France into town, Boardman broke Graeme Obree's world hour record. This time Chris and his mentor Peter Keen had been able to use the power meter as part of the event preparation, and so for the first time we were able to measure exactly how hard you have to ride to break a world record.

Having looked at where my understanding and use of the power meter originated, let me now speed into the future to consider how your power meter will evolve. The power meters of the future will rely on built-in sensors so that you remain unaware of their presence until you switch on your data receiver. Innovative companies such as Stages have already started to make their power meters on this basis. Unlike the present, your power meter sensors will be located so that you will be able to measure how hard you are riding even after you have swapped your wheels or even changed your whole bike. Indeed, it's likely that all the contact points between you and your bike, and your bike and the road, will be instrumented: saddle, handlebars,

left and right arms and legs, and front and back tyres. These developments are largely hardware based and much of the necessary technology is already available. Instrumenting your bike in this way and gathering the resulting data is therefore feasible, at least in theory, with sufficient resources and the right 'know how'. But while the hardware advances will enable you to measure more, the really exciting advances lie in the information to be extracted from these measurements and how it will help you.

Unlike the present, the power meter of the future will know more about your cycling than you and your coach. With access to so many measurements, it will become your friendly resident cycling expert. This expert will be able to guide you in all aspects of how to most effectively set up, pedal and train on your bike. Your power meter's expertise will lie in its software and the data it gathers on you and your bike. The input from you will be minimal (apart from the effort involved in riding your bike). It will provide a comprehensive analysis of your every pedal revolution. If you want to know that your riding position is correct, take a short video clip with your phone while you ride for a few minutes on your indoor trainer. By scanning your image and using its sensors, your power meter will be able to find the optimal position for you as you ride. If you want to check that you are pedalling efficiently, your power meter will give you immediate feedback on your cycling technique and how to improve it. If you want to know how hard you have to ride to complete a 25-mile time trial in under an hour or an alpine sportive within the time limit, your power meter will calculate it and show you. If you are wondering whether changing equipment will allow you to ride faster, put your power meter into equipment testing mode and it will tell you.

Your biggest gains will come from your power meter's expert guidance once you start training. After your first training ride, your power meter will start analysing your training data. It will then use this to calculate your expected performance changes. It will not stop there though. Crunching through large amounts of data is something that computers do much more effectively than humans. It will identify patterns and relationships in your training data in a way that outperforms the capabilities of even the best cycle coach. As a consequence of its analysis of your previous training sessions, your power meter will also be able to advise you on what to do next. Using a power meter in the future will mean you have no need to worry about when, how long or how hard you should train. Your power meter will be able to calculate all this for you, based on analysis of your own personal training data.

Once you start a training session, your power meter will guide you along the way with more than route navigation. It will be able to prescribe your training intensity moment by moment, like a coach instructing you: go harder up here, pedal easier down there, hold this effort for another mile, and then pedal easily to recover. At the end of your training session, you'll get immediate feedback on how well you have trained. Finally, your power meter will calculate when you should next ride for maximum training benefit.

The expert power meter of the future may sound rather fanciful, but my current research is focused on making this a reality. Reaching this future was precisely what first motivated me to study sports science more than twenty-five years ago. For many of the intervening years the way forward has not always been clear. But now advances in technology, my current research and the experience gained along the way suggest this future is not so far off. I am confident that you will not have to wait another quarter of a century to experience some form of expert power meter.

As I return to the present, it is clear that there is a training predicament. The science behind cycle training and racing has advanced considerably in the past twenty years. Now you can measure accurately what happens during training and racing directly from your bike. The Internet provides a significant repository of power meter files from a wide range of different cycling events for you to learn from. But your power meter is not yet smart enough to make this process really simple and do all the analysis for you. One day, power meters will provide a complete expert solution for bike training and racing. But with a little knowledge you can already easily use your power meter to help you make better decisions about your training and racing. From my experience and research, there are plenty of simple things that you can do to make your training with a power meter more effective. This book will tell you how.

CHAPTER ONE

AN OVERVIEW OF TRAINING WITH POWER METERS

I have been privileged to learn a lot by working with elite riders and their coaches during my career. In particular, I have seen first hand how Britain's elite cycling programme has developed from a struggling minority sport to one of the most successful in the world. The concepts behind this success are very simple: clear goal setting and good planning. Anyone who is familiar with the success that Britain's best cyclists have achieved will tell you this. You can do this too and benefit in the same way with your training. I am afraid this does not mean that you *will* become an Olympic or Tour de France champion. But if you have ambition, use goal setting and plan your training effectively, I am confident that you will be surprised by what you can achieve.

This book is about training and using a power meter to help translate your goals and plans into improved performance. It does not matter *why* you train – you should still find the information relevant as long as you are motivated to improve. Your current level of fitness and how far you are able to progress are not important. From my experience I have found it impossible to tell how far an individual can improve. I have on several occasions helped riders achieve new PBs after they have been told they

have reached the limits of their potential. Using your power meter can help you find that extra little bit. Used thoughtfully it is a potent training tool. But it is important to recognize that it is *how*, not *whether*, you use it that makes the difference. Your power meter can help you in many aspects of your training, from preparation and planning beforehand, to monitoring and analysis afterwards. It acts like a magnifying glass with which to examine your training.

THIS BOOK

Getting the most from training with your power meter is about much more than what you do on your bike. The process begins before you start your training session and continues after you have stopped riding. Your power meter can help you develop, analyse and refine your whole training strategy. But to do so you need to have a training strategy and a reasonable grasp of the fundamental principles of training.

Having a training strategy means that you approach your training in a thoughtful manner. It also implies that you continually seek ways to improve your training. Grasping the fundamental principles of training is about learning to manage your training, not about becoming a coach. Although I do suggest you seek the support of a coach if you really want to push your limits, for the purposes of this book I am going to assume that you are coaching yourself.

Regardless of whether or not you have a coach, to use a power meter well it is helpful to understand the principles of the training process. The difference between being a rider and a coach is analogous to being a car driver or a mechanic on a long road trip. To complete the journey you do not need a mechanic's detailed understanding of how your car's engine works – you just have to be able to drive your car (or in this case ride your bike) to your destination.

Your training strategy can be thought of as a three-step process. First you set your *goals*, next you *plan* your training programme, and after training you *evaluate* and refine your training programme. At each of these three steps your power meter can help refine the process.

Developing your training strategy is a straightforward process but there are some guidelines worth following to make the most of your training. Start by setting yourself goals that you then use to plan and programme your training. Review the strengths and weaknesses in your current level of fitness or performance, and take into account the time and any other resources you need for training. This information provides the key components to planning your training programme. Once you have written out your programme and started training, resist the temptation to follow it too rigidly. Check routinely that you are training as intended and that the effects are as expected. Keep looking for ways to improve your training further.

Training with your power meter helps you implement this strategy in many ways. Your goals can be set in quantifiable terms so that you can specify precisely the details of your training. Before your training begins you can plan the specific power output at which you intend to train and for how long, given any type of session. During the training session your power meter can act to remind you of these training targets and to provide immediate feedback on where you are relative to them. And after your training session you will be able to check that you were actually hitting the numbers you planned. With a little experience you will be able to use your power meter to obtain objective assessments of your strengths and weaknesses in training and racing.

Training with a power meter is also a journey of self-discovery. For example, you will learn how hard you can work from the start of a session, and you will be able to see the consequences in terms of your power output, speed, heart rate and effort. With a power meter, pacing your effort in training and races becomes more measured and controlled. Over time the cumulative benefit of training with a power meter should be apparent as it shows you how your fitness has changed.

Keeping the principles of training in mind will help guide you in your training. The theory of training based around overload, recovery, overcompensation and progression is straightforward (covered in more depth in Chapter 4). You can use your power meter to ensure that your training overload is appropriate and that your recovery is sufficient. You can use Training Intensity Bands (TIBs) to structure your training and guide the use of your power meter out on the road. Using TIBs in your training provides a simple scheme for you to specify and

With a little experience you will be able to use your power meter to obtain objective assessments of your strengths and weaknesses in training and racing.

monitor your target power output in every training session. It makes communication and planning around your training easier, too. If your training progresses well, your power meter will display clear signs of overcompensation in your fitness. Equally, analysis of your power meter data can help identify signs of staleness and overtraining if things are not quite right.

This brief overview has set out the broad strategy for this book. I aim to help you think about your cycling goals, your plans to achieve them and, of course, how training with a power meter can underpin your success. In the next chapter I will explore the relationship between work and power, and why you measure these on your bike.

CHAPTER TWO

THE POWER METER

WORK AND POWER: HOW IT'S ALL ABOUT THE RATE

You are familiar I'm sure with the concept that when you do work, whether it is lifting weights or training on your bike, you use energy. The more work you do, the more energy you burn. When you have finished working you eat food and replace the energy you have used. Energy and work are measured in joules (or its equivalent in calories). Your power meter measures how much work you do on your bike but you should not normally be particularly interested in this. Instead, you should prefer to focus on the rate at which you work or, to use its proper name, power.

Let us examine in a little more detail why you are not primarily interested in measuring the joules or calories you use in training on your bike. Imagine there is a wheelbarrow full of rocks that weigh the same as you and you have been challenged to move them to the top of a hill. It is quite a bit of work (or energy) to get those rocks to the hilltop. In fact, you can calculate quite accurately exactly how many joules are involved in this challenge. All you need to do is measure the weight of your rocks and

the height of the hill, and multiply them (by gravity, which is the force we are overcoming in this example). The physics of calculating the amount of work you do when cycling up the hill are exactly the same: it is also the product of your weight (the same as the rocks), the height of the hill and gravity. I have used this example as it does not matter whether you are considering moving your rocks up the hill or cycling up the hill: the work required in both examples is the same.

When you are halfway up the hill you notice other people have taken the same challenge (you can choose now whether you prefer to think in terms of rocks or cycling). Not wanting to be outdone, you work harder to speed up. With considerable extra effort, you manage to get to the top first. Now let us compare the work of getting to halfway nice and steadily with that of getting from halfway to the top as fast you can. Was it the same (as you travelled half the hill each time) or was it different (the second half felt much more stressful as you pushed harder)?

This question is about the amount of work (or energy) you used. Comparing the work of getting from the bottom to halfway with halfway to the top gives the

Measuring your work rate when you train is the primary function of your power meter.

same result: it is half the hill both times. So when you are cycling up a hill, how fast you climb it does not change the total amount of work you do. To increase the amount of work you would either have to move more rocks (in other words put weight on) or pick a higher hill. Even then you probably would not mind the extra work too much, as long as you can compensate by taking a little longer. The point of this example is that knowing the total amount of work you complete does not tell you how hard you have been working. So what is the reason that the second half of the hill felt much harder? It is because you increased the rate or the speed at which you went up hill. You did the same amount of work but faster, or in other words you increased your work rate. Increasing your work rate is what this book is all about!

Measuring your work rate when you train is the primary function of your power meter. Power is the measurement of work rate. Your power output is measured in watts (W). You may be familiar with the watt as a measure of power output in other contexts too, as it is the standard way of quanti-fying power output. A number of household devices use watts to describe how powerful they are or the rate at which they consume energy – Table 1 has some examples. Somebody (or something) with a high power output can do a lot of work very fast.

On your bike you are the engine. Your power output is a measure of the engine size with which you propel your bike. The higher your power output, the bigger your engine and the faster you go. Your power output is determined by two factors: the force with which you press on your pedals and your cadence (how fast you spin your pedals). You can increase your power output by pressing harder on your pedals. Alternatively, pedalling faster with the same force will also increase your power output.

There is a direct relationship between your pedal force, your cadence and your power output. This relationship means that you can use different combinations of pedal force and cadence to produce the same power output. For example, you could produce the same training power output with a low cadence and high pedal forces, or with a high cadence and low pedal forces.

Table 1. HOW DO YOU COMPARE?

	Maximum Power (W)	On a bike
Light bulb	100	Easy ride
Television	170	Medium ride
Computer	200	Tempo ride
Large television	280	Elite race
Microwave	800	Team pursuit
Drill	900	Women's road sprint
Electric hob ring	1400	Men's road sprint
Kettle	2200	Track sprint
Washing machine	3000	Standing start

You might consider the implications of this for your training.

There is another important point about the relationship between pedal force, cadence and power output that you will notice when you are out on your bike: this is what happens to your power output when you stop pedalling, in other words when you freewheel. Because power output is a measure of work *rate*, when you stop pedalling it immediately falls to zero. Equally, if you do not apply any force to the pedals (for example if your chain comes off), your power output again falls to zero.

WHY USE A POWER METER?

Given the range of different devices that are available to help you record your training, you may wonder why you should consider using a power meter. Using a bike computer to monitor your training time and distance provides a much cheaper alternative, so could it prove equivalent? The short answer is 'no'. Currently there is no alternative to the power meter that provides as much or as important information for your training. This is a key question so I will explain more fully.

In order to train effectively it is helpful to plan and monitor your training intensity.

First consider what can be measured without a power meter. There are many training devices that enable you to record your basic training outcomes. Whilst out on your bike you can easily monitor simple variables such as your training time, distance, speed and even metres climbed. To do this there is a wide range of devices available including bike computers, GPS devices and so on. If you have a smartphone you can probably install a cheap or free app to record these too. It is also comparatively straightforward to obtain a more detailed recording of your training incorporating more technical variables such as your cadence and heart rate. Typically, both these measurements will require you to purchase additional equipment or sensors specifically for the purpose. Even so, this equipment is still relatively affordable for most people. Given that you can easily measure such a number of training variables, going to further trouble and expense in order to measure power output might seem superfluous. Let us explore why training with a power meter can be sufficiently useful to justify the extra cost.

In order to train effectively it is helpful to plan and monitor how hard you work in each training session, otherwise known as your training intensity. The more detailed reasons for this and other principles of training I will discuss in the subsequent chapters. As you work harder on your bike you will go faster and therefore cover more distance. So you could use training time, distance and speed in order to monitor and evaluate your training intensity. Indeed, many people have and continue to use these measures very successfully to inform their training practice. But if you have tried monitoring your training distance and speed in the past, you will already know

the limitation of using these measurements to gauge how hard you have worked in training. Your training distance and speed are not only related to how hard you train. Several other factors also exert a powerful influence over how far or fast you can ride. These factors include variables such as air pressure, humidity and temperature, wind speed and direction, the road gradient and road surface characteristics, your riding position and your clothing. Importantly, most of these factors can change continuously throughout a ride and these changes are not easy to measure. It is impractical to try and take account of these changes in order to plan your training based simply on speed or distance. Equally, you may want to monitor and evaluate your training over a period of time, but it is often almost impossible to calculate whether the change in your training speed between two sessions was due to a difference in how hard you worked, or a change in one or more of the variables above.

Using a power meter removes this uncertainty. By training with a power meter you can quantify precisely how hard you are working at any given moment regardless of the terrain and other environmental conditions. After your training is complete, your power output data provides the basis for a simple comparison with previous sessions. You can determine easily whether you achieved the desired training intensity. You can even calculate whether any changes in how fast or far you trained were due to variation in your fitness, training intensity, or the terrain or other environmental factors.

In addition to power output, you can gauge how hard you are working by measuring your heart rate. Although training by heart rate is not the same as measuring power output, it is worth discussing further. The reason for considering this is that a heart rate monitor measures something quite different from a bike computer or GPS device, and the combination of a power meter and heart rate monitor is better than either on its own. Bike computers and GPS devices record how far and fast you went in your training session. Using a heart rate monitor will tell you about how hard your body is working. Knowing how hard your body is working tells you your training intensity. Therefore, when you train with a heart rate monitor you do not need to be concerned about how your speed is affected by wind, hills or road surface. This is because you can plan based on a target training intensity rather than speed or distance. Regardless of whether you are grinding uphill or coasting downhill, battling headwinds or floating on tailwinds, you can easily focus on hitting your target training intensity if it is specified by your heart rate not your speed.

Training with a heart rate monitor is a little like using your rev meter when driving your car: you can use it to provide some idea of the stress on your engine. In the case of cycling you are the engine and your heart rate shows how stressed you are. Consequently many athletes, and not just riders, consider a heart rate monitor to be an indispensable training tool. But whilst a heart rate monitor alone can prove a very useful training tool, when it is combined with a power meter an even more comprehensive insight into your training is possible.

Your power meter measures the work rate your body sustains in training, whilst your heart rate monitor tells you how stressful your body finds this work rate. Thus the power output is a measure of the demands of the training session, whilst your heart rate is a reflection of your body's response to or capacity to cope with this training demand. Being able to compare training demands and responses is another of the key benefits from using a power meter. Knowing you trained at 150W for an hour tells you a lot about your training session and fitness. If you also measured your heart rate response to it you can learn even more. For example, riding at 150W may have initially elicited a heart rate of 180bpm. But perhaps after few weeks of training your heart rate response to the same session has dropped to 170bpm. This drop in your heart rate indicates that you are getting fitter and confirms your training is working. Training with your power meter or heart rate monitor alone would not have enabled you to detect this improvement.

When you can specify training session demands and measure the resulting response in this way, you are able to replicate some important aspects of laboratory-based fitness testing. In some situations it is still useful to be able to have the tight control provided by the laboratory environment for specialist exercise tests. But in many cases being able to evaluate cycling performance out on the road as it happens and where it matters is more useful. Fitting a power meter to your bike turns it into a mobile laboratory. As you get fitter you will be able to see it in the power output you can produce when you race or train hard. You can also compare how your body responds to a specific work rate. If your speed is lower in training, a quick look at your power output will tell you whether it is because you are not trying hard enough or because the conditions are tough. Similarly, when you record a PB your power meter will help you decide whether it was because the conditions were faster or because your fitness has improved.

Training with a power meter shows you unequivocally your improvements in fitness as an increase in your training power output. When you can produce a higher power output you know you will be able to ride faster. Moreover you can tell this simply by looking at your power meter data during and after a ride. With this information available to you, there is no need to go to the laboratory to measure changes in your fitness. Instead you can look at the power output you can produce for a specific effort, or measure your heart rate response to a fixed power output. Being able to measure that your training is progressing is highly motivating. It tells you your training is effective, and enhances your focus and desire to persist as you feel the effort is worthwhile. As a consequence you can continue to push yourself in training. This is why monitoring and evaluating your sessions is such an important part of your training strategy. When you are struggling in training you should rapidly be able to spot the emerging downward trend from session to session. Even if your power meter cannot tell you what to do, knowing that you need to make a change is helpful.

Power meters are particularly useful in goal setting and planning. For your goals and planning, you want to know where your fitness is at present and can plan where it needs to be in the future. In this way you can prepare for a forthcoming event knowing exactly what you need to achieve and where you are on the road to achieving it. Using your power meter, you can set yourself a goal based on your power output for a target training session. Then you can use your power meter to track your progress in training towards being able to hit that power output for the session. In this way you will also be able to gauge directly from your training whether you are ready to complete your event.

As an illustration, imagine that your dream is to do well in an Olympic-distance triathlon. You are confident of your run if you can be near the front at the end of the bike leg. You convert this dream into your training goal by specifying the power output you would be satisfied with for the bike leg. Extrapolating from this, you decide that if you are able to produce 270W for one hour in training then when you race you should be able to start the run in the position you want to be. Now your goal has been set, your training has a real focus. Whenever you want to check how your training is progressing, riding at 270W will let you know. The fact that you train on different roads to the triathlon itself is not an issue in measuring your progress either. Finally, during the event itself your power meter can help you execute your race strategy. With your power meter in view you can judge your effort carefully, regardless of your speed, the terrain and the wind.

IS IT FOR YOU?

Although I think that using a power meter can be straightforward, I would also suggest that it does not work well for everyone. When examined in detail cycling becomes surprisingly complex, training even more so. Using a power meter extends your potential to identify, quantify and analyse the detail of this complexity. You may welcome the opportunity to understand a little more clearly what's happening in the complicated picture of your training. But for some people this does not appeal, and they do not enjoy or even want to look at their training in this way.

TYPES OF POWER METERS

The range of power meters on the market today is changing rapidly. A benefit of this development is that the price of power meters is falling too. Innovative companies such as Stages are able to design and sell power meters at a price that brings them within the reach of the keen cyclist. Because of the range of different power meters that are now available, I will not review them here individually.

Most power meters use strain gauges to measure the forces that you are applying to your bike. Different manufacturers have approached this challenge in different ways. The German power meter manufacturer SRM were the first to make a commercially available power meter and this is built into the chainset. Consequently it is able to measure the power you produce with both legs before it goes through your chain to your back wheel.

Several manufacturers produce power meters that work on a similar principle. PowerTap locate their strain gauges in the rear hub. With this method your

power output is measured after your chain drive. This should in theory result in them reading a tiny bit lower than those meters that measure before the chain drive. Other approaches that have been taken include measuring your power output directly from your chain and your bottom bracket axle.

Perhaps the most interesting approach to power meters is to locate the force sensors in your pedal or shoe. The technical challenges of doing this in a robust and reliable manner are significant. Once overcome, this approach promises benefits both in terms of ease of use and the potential to analyse your pedalling style in much greater detail. For example, it will be possible to tell where in the pedal cycle you generate your force and to compare the power output of your left and right legs separately. In contrast, the Stages power meter measures power output from your left crank only and doubles this to predict your power output from both legs. This approach keeps their device simpler and therefore cheaper to produce.

Throughout this book I make regular reference to strategy, numbers, figures and analysis. Training with your power meter helps inform this approach. If this perspective makes sense to you and you tend to prefer a structured and organized environment, you will likely enjoy using a power meter. But if you are less keen on numbers and figures, or they have little relevance to you, then you may also find training with a power meter unintuitive and unappealing. Riders enjoy cycling for many different

reasons. For some, measuring and critically evaluating their work rate is not part of that motivation. I find riding a bike expresses a spirit of freedom and adventure, rhythm and feel. I can appreciate that some riders find this compromised when it is analysed with a power meter.

Whatever your philosophy and perspective on cycling, I do encourage you to ensure that your power meter does not dictate all your rides.

SRM Power Meter.
(SRM)

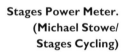

Stages Power Meter.
(Michael Stowe/
Stages Cycling)

STARTING TRAINING WITH A POWER METER

Once you have decided to take the plunge and invest in a power meter, how do you get started? What should you do first? How do you make sense of the plethora of data that you will rapidly accumulate from every ride? Here I will examine just the broader strategy, then in subsequent chapters I will look at the specifics of how you implement the strategy.

The first thing to ensure after you have fitted your power meter is that you know how to calibrate it. This might sound obvious, but if you are going to spend any time at all looking at the data from your training you want to make sure that it is accurate. Data from an uncalibrated power meter is only good for the rubbish bin. The calibration method you need to use will be specific to your power meter. Be sure

25

to read this bit of the manual carefully and make sure you understand the process fully. If you are at all unsure, contact someone who knows what to do, such as your power meter manufacturer or the shop where you bought it, or hunt on the Internet for further guidance.

Calibrate your power meter regularly, if possible before every ride. In this way you should quickly get to know both the procedure and the calibration figures that are typical of your device. Look out for situations where your power meter will not calibrate easily or suddenly starts giving unusual calibration readings. Treat these situations with suspicion. Depending on your power meter, it may simply be a sign that a battery needs replacing. But be aware that a full manufacturer's service or recalibration can be required after a year or two of heavy use. Do not skimp on this if you have good reason to suspect it is required. Try to ensure you have a fully functioning and accurately calibrated power meter before you hit the road. If you and a friend have a different power meter, compare the two on one bike; you then have a useful benchmark to check against if you are concerned that either is not reading correctly.

Before you start training consider the data storage interval that is set on your power meter. Most power meters enable you to change how frequently your data is stored. Typically, the options to store data vary from every 0.5 to 30 seconds. Storing data every half a second will give you a highly detailed picture of how your power output changes throughout your ride. Every slight change in power output will be recorded and result in a very 'noisy' graph of your training session. With these noisy graphs it can be difficult to follow the general trends in your data for that ride. The other negative

aspect of using a short recording interval is that you will fill the memory of your power meter more quickly. Depending on the specification of your power meter, its memory may become full and cease to record before you complete your training. On the other hand, long data storage intervals mean that your training data gets averaged over long time periods. This has the effect of flattening out the variations in your recorded power output. It makes the overall trend for that ride very clear but without some of the smaller changes in power output that might be important to you.

Imagine you complete a 10 second sprint and then freewheel for 10 seconds before resuming your normal riding. With your power meter set to record every 0.5 seconds you will see your large (hopefully) surge in power output as your sprint begins. Then at the end of the sprint you will see your power output fall to zero watts (0W) before rising again as you resume riding normally. However, when your power meter is set to average data over 30 seconds you will see none of this. Instead you will just record one value that represents the combined average of your sprint, freewheel and normal riding sections. If you wanted to know what your peak sprint power output was you would be annoyed to find that this was not recorded.

The best strategy is to use the shortest data-recording interval you can safely manage whilst ensuring that your power meter's memory will not become full before the end of your ride. Most software for analysing data from your power meter will have a smoothing feature built in so that you can see the overall trend in your data more clearly if you wish. By using a short data-recording interval you should always be able to zoom in on any sections of your training that are of particular interest to examine them in extra detail.

Part of the beauty of using a power meter is that, once it is fitted and functioning correctly, it just sits there unobtrusively measuring and recording everything. For your first few sessions you don't need to do anything other than continue your training as normal. As you get used to having power output figures to review, new insights may start to emerge. A common observation is that your power output drops towards the end of your training efforts or sessions. To counter this, when you train with your power meter you can use it to pace your training more effectively. In the early part of your next ride try holding back and limiting your work rate to only a little above the average of the previous session. As a consequence you should find that you are able to sustain your training power output right through until the end without fading. There have been several research studies that show redistributing your effort in this way improves your overall power output and performance.

A different way you can develop your training with a power meter is to try and nudge higher your power output for a specific training section or session. The first time you do this, ride in a restrained manner leaving plenty in reserve. Each subsequent time you repeat the same training session, try to nudge your power output up a tiny bit. This type of training really makes the most of training with a power meter. Be mindful, though, that it quickly becomes very demanding mentally and physically. Without a power meter you would have to resort to using your training time or speed which are too susceptible to changes in the direction and strength of the wind to be useful in the same way.

Once you return home you can download your training file and 'relive' your ride. It is at home after a training session that the fun and added insight gained from using a power meter can really start. After your ride you will be able to look at plots of how your power output, speed, cadence and heart rate changed throughout the ride. You should also be able to zoom in on sections of particular interest from your ride. It may be a particular climb, an interval session or a crucial part of a race. You can use websites such as Strava and Map My Tracks to monitor your performance over regular training segments. Soon you'll find you start to 'think in watts'. As you become more familiar with your power output it will become your benchmark for analysing a session, rather than looking at your speed or heart rate. By comparing your training rides and race performances in this way you will be better able to observe how your fitness changes over time. Then you will progress to using the numbers from these post-ride analyses to set training goals, to monitor your progress and as the basis for further projects.

Right from the start establish a system for managing your training files. Keep your file system simple and logical as you are likely to be using it a lot and over time you are going to amass a lot of training files. Finding the ones you want becomes frustrating if you have allowed your files to become strewn around your computer or, worse, over several computers. Many power meters come with software to help keep your files organized. This tends to make the software worth installing for this purpose alone. Don't forget to backup your files too. A broken computer is bad enough, but losing years' of training data at the same time can be even worse. A useful tip is to upload your

It is at home after a training session that the fun and added insight gained from using a power meter can really start.

data to one or more of the online websites. Several, such as Garmin, Strava and Map My Tracks, offer a free service and allow you to share your rides with others. By doing this you are also backing-up your training to several different places should the worst happen.

REMOVE THE GUESSWORK

A power meter is one of the most advanced training tools available, but using one effectively is nonetheless straightforward. Whilst power meters are not yet as smart as I predict they will become in the first chapter, you do not need to be a scientist to use one. Your power meter can be used merely to record your bike training. You can do this

SOFTWARE AND WEBSITES

In order to analyse your power meter data you are likely to have three options: software bundled with your power meter, standalone software, and a web-based data service.

Bundled software has the advantage of being free and usually has the ability to download your data onto your own computer. This means that it will work wherever you are and that you can retain control of your data. Bundled software normally allows you to configure the settings on your power meter too. The level of data analysis varies but the methods of data analysis discussed in this book are usually possible.

Standalone software can be obtained as commercial packages or, as with Golden Cheetah, as a free download. One of the advantages of standalone packages is that they tend to provide you with a more sophisticated level of analysis for your power meter data. Some software packages will also be able to download data from your power meter directly, provided you have a popular device, but there is no guarantee of this so check first if this feature is important to you. Standalone packages also tend to give you some control over your power meter data, although again there is considerable variability in the extent to which you can keep control of how your data is obtained and how much of it can be analysed or exported from the software.

The third option is to upload your power meter data to a web-based service. There are a number of websites offering free data upload and data analysis. Many of these sites offer basic analysis for free and a more advanced analysis at a cost. With this approach you often benefit from rapid access to the more cutting-edge methods of analysing your power meter data. The services tend to work well for the most popular models of power meter and data logger. Of course, to use these services you need access to an internet connection whenever you want to upload or review your data. You usually also have to give up some control over your power meter data. For example, you may find the upload system does not enable you to store your power meter data files on your own computer system, and bulk export of all your data from the web service may not be possible at all or not in a convenient file format. The implication of this is that backup of your data, or conducting your own more personal analysis of your raw data, becomes difficult.

Another aspect of web-based services is that once your data are uploaded to a website it can be very easy to 'share' or compare the details of your rides with friends and team mates. This often means you can join virtual online competitions, challenges and league tables. For example several websites will automatically scan your power meter and GPS data to see if you have ridden an identified 'segment'. This segment often takes the form of a hill climb or someone's favourite road or circuit. Once found, your time and power output for the segment are posted to create a league table enabling you to see how you compare against other riders. Perhaps more usefully these sites show you how your current ride compares with previous rides, enabling you to track changes in your fitness based upon your performance on your favourite segments.

without complicated planning or analysis, and you can get started right away. In fact on your first rides this is exactly how I suggest you use it. However, if you wish to exploit your power meter's full potential to help you in your training there is much more that you can use it for.

Your power meter can help you remove much of the guesswork around your training. Exactly how much guesswork is removed is down to you. As with many things in life, you can get more out of using your power meter by investing a little time and effort in its use. The good news is that the simpler things will probably yield the biggest benefits to your training. The law of diminishing returns applies here. Once

you start using your power meter to tackle more advanced and sophisticated projects, it signifies that you have mastered the initial steps, and it is probably also a sign that you are hunting for smaller gains. This law of diminishing returns means that you can realize much of the benefit of using a power meter by mastering the essentials. Beyond this, the sophistication of your approach can be dictated by your interest and desire to seek further gains.

In this book I aim to cover the essentials and keep things reasonably simple. Once you start looking for smaller incremental benefits then it is time to call in or become an expert.

CHAPTER THREE

PLANNING TRAINING WITH POWER METERS

The principles for getting the most from training with your power meter are really quite straightforward. You just need to have a training strategy and then use your power meter as an integral part of it. Using your power meter effectively really is this simple. It is about bringing an extra level of detail to your training planning and analysis. Of course the planning begins well before you start riding your bike, and remember that your power meter is just one of the tools in your training toolkit, albeit an important one.

Successful training is not an automatic consequence of training with a power meter; success comes from using it as part of a wider training strategy that you have developed. Therefore in this chapter I will focus on what a training strategy is and how training with a power meter can be part of it. By the end of this chapter you should be able to start applying these essentials to your own training. Once you have a training strategy and are using your power meter as part of it, you have conquered the essentials. Beyond this you are progressing to elaborating and refining your strategy.

TRAINING WITH A STRATEGY

The principles of a good training strategy are simple. They can be summarized by the following three points:

1. **Goals**: identify the outcomes you intend from your training
2. **Plan**: create a plan and train to a programme
3. **Evaluate**: monitor, evaluate and refine your training plan.

I have worked with some outstanding riders who despite producing impressive performances still sometimes feel that they are not in control of their fitness. They have spent hundreds of hours training for specific competitions. They are dedicated to training hard and improving their cycling performance. But their peak form seems to come and go of its own accord. This happens despite their best efforts to dictate it in training. This scenario is not uncommon, especially with riders who race regularly. It can happen regardless of whether the rider trains with a power meter, too. Typically, the issue relates to what the riders do before they start training, rather than what they are doing during it. Usually these riders have a training programme but, when asked about their training strategy, their goals, their plan and their evaluation, they quickly start back pedalling.

Many riders invest significantly in their cycling; probably, as you are reading this book, you do too (or at least the person who gave you the book thinks you do). If you have or are thinking of training with a power meter you will probably spend considerable time, money and effort pursuing your dreams on a bike. But do you train with some kind of strategy? A training strategy encourages you to think about what you want to train for and creates opportunities for you to focus and improve your performance. This in turn shapes how you can use your power meter. Your training strategy helps guide the whole process of training, not just the programme itself. It provides a quick and easy structure that leads from why you train in the first place to analysing what you have done. Perhaps you cycle for fun and are concerned that a training strategy may make it less enjoyable. Rest assured, your strategy can and should be simple. The process of developing a training strategy can be fun. And getting more from your training because your plan has come to fruition is doubly rewarding.

If you are serious about improving your cycling then there are no two ways about it: you should have goals, you should plan what you do, and you should evaluate it afterwards. That is a training strategy. If you do already have a strategy, then 'well done'. My experience is that many riders do not. You can skim through the rest of this section knowing you are already ahead of the peloton.

If you do not have a training strategy, stop and ask yourself why. Perhaps you know you should be more strategic in your training but do not get around to acting on it? Or maybe you are just not sure what to do. If you are in the first group, ask yourself if you really are concerned with improving your cycling. If not then this book may provide some useful tips for getting a little more from your training. If you are serious about improving, you need to change! Identify your goals, plan what you need to do and evaluate your training subsequently. It is an easy and straightforward process but it can really pay off in terms of helping you find that little bit extra.

One other thing I suggest as your continue this book is that you take a just few minutes to write down the key points of your own strategy. It does not matter whether the changes you are looking to make are large or small – just write them down. I'm sure you will find it helpful. Now, let us consider goal setting, planning and evaluation, the three elements of your strategy, in a little more detail.

Goal setting

Goal setting is the first part of a good training strategy, regardless of whether or not you train with a power meter. Once integrated appropriately into your training with a power meter, goal setting is one of the most effective ways of enhancing your performance. However, many riders struggle to set appropriate goals, so I will look at how this is done.

First you need to know the difference between your dreams and your goals. In particular, it is important that you set yourself goals over which you have control. For maximum benefit I suggest that you set incremental goals that are based around your training and have a deadline attached.

Once you have set out your long-term goals you may also want to break these down into some short-term ones too. Later in this section I will go into a little more detail on goal setting as I think it is fundamental to training with a power meter effectively. If you are already well versed in goal setting then you may want to skip this section or just consider the example I give in the Chapter 11 on further training.

There is an enormous body of research that shows that if you work towards specified goals you will perform better. World-leading psychologists Professors Edwin Locke and Gary Latham established the theory of goal setting in 1990. They based their theory on the findings of more than 400 scientific studies. The professors found that appropriate goal setting has a number of important benefits. Your goals can lead you to make greater effort and to be more persistent; they serve to direct your attention, effort and action towards your training; they reduce the influence of inevitable distractions; they enable you to make the most of your current ability; and they also motivate you to develop new skills and fitness. Goal setting almost sounds like a magic potion – why would you not want to embrace a training strategy that involves this?

If you use your power meter to try and maintain a particular power output in training then you are working towards a goal. Without this goal your use of your power meter might be limited to recording what you do. You can use your power meter to help provide the focus and motivation for your training session. As a consequence you will probably train harder and this is what appropriate goal setting provides. By identifying and setting your goals you create your focus and a commitment in your training.

Without goals your training can still be enjoyable and rewarding, but it cannot be quite as focused. Nor will your motivation to persevere in difficult sessions be as great.

As a lot has been written on the importance of setting goals, I am going to presume that you do not need to be persuaded further. The most important thing about goal setting is that you do it, as it is all too easy to continue training without identifying goals. The challenge is to set your goals appropriately. At first this may seem more complicated than you think. I see experienced athletes and coaches make mistakes with their goal setting. The good news is that by concentrating on training with your power meter you can help simplify this process. In fact an important benefit of training with a power meter is that it encourages you to train in a goal-oriented manner. It also gives you greater scope and flexibility with your goals. Building your goals around training with your power meter can lead to very effective goal setting. As a consequence some common mistakes can be avoided simply by setting your goal in terms of training with your power meter. It starts with knowing your goals from your dreams.

YOUR DREAMS, YOUR GOALS AND KEEPING CONTROL

Psychologists have found that regularly spending time imagining yourself achieving your dreams does not lead to you performing well. The likelihood is that what you dream about achieving on your bike is not on the whole within your control. Spending time thinking about this does not help you get the job done – quite the reverse. This is why your dreams or similar inspirations do not make appropriate goals. Instead you need to focus on outcomes that are dictated by you and the effort you make. You can determine your goals, unlike your dreams. Therefore the key to appropriate goal setting is to differentiate between your training goals and your cycling dreams. Your dreams are things that, whilst they may inspire you, provide no day-to-day focus. The latter is the job of a training goal. Goals are clear, measurable objectives with a specific time frame. If you are working towards something that lacks these characteristics then it is not a goal, or at the very least needs to be worked into an effective goal.

Below are examples of the kinds of riders' dreams I commonly encounter.

Dream 1: Improving your health and fitness
How attractive the new slimmer, fitter you will be after training.

Dream 2: Taking on a challenging event
Soaring up the last climb to complete a mountainous sportive just like the winner in the Tour de France.

Dream 3: Competing
Winning a race by edging out a rival on the line, or reaching a particular level of recognition or status in cycling.

The important thing to recognize is that these statements are dreams, they are not training goals. In Chapter 11 I will return to these dreams to show how they can be recast as appropriate goals, but here I will focus next on my simple rule for goal setting.

SETTING INCREMENTAL TRAINING GOALS TO A DEADLINE
Earlier I said that one of the most effective ways to enhance your performance is to integrate goal setting into your training with a power meter. This above all else in this book *will* produce results. To benefit from this you need clear and effective goals that are challenging and motivating. My simple rule for goal setting is as follows: set incremental training goals with a deadline. Training with your power meter to pursue goals set in this way becomes straightforward. There are three key aspects to this rule:

1. Set goals relating to your training and preparation, rather than your ultimate outcome such as a competition or event.
2. Set your goals incrementally, or with a specified improvement, whenever possible.
3. Identify a deadline or target date for reaching your training goal.

SETTING TRAINING GOALS
The reason you set goals is because they help provide motivation, focus and challenge for you in your endeavours. When you race or take part in an event you are there to compete, whether it is against others or just yourself. Performing well in an event relies on how well you have prepared and how well you execute your strategy on the day. Being at the event and taking part is in itself likely to provide you with sufficient motivation, focus and challenge. Therefore the primary benefits of goal setting are likely to arise from linking your goals to your training rather than to competition. In addition, goals linked to your training are more likely to be under your control compared with those for an event or competition.

SETTING INCREMENTAL GOALS
When I worked at British Cycling alongside Sir Dave Brailsford, he regularly promoted the concept of 'aggregation of marginal gains'. His philosophy was simple: everyone should look for small (marginal) ways to improve the team's performance. Once

these small individual gains were aggregated, they might amount to a substantial performance improvement. Sir Dave had the right idea, but his marginal gain philosophy is limited. He should be looking for *incremental* gains, not marginal ones. Seeking incremental gains means you are always looking to improve on your current level of performance. Incremental goals by their very nature will become challenging as you always seek ways to go one better. Incremental training goals enable you to exploit the principle of progression discussed in the next chapter.

There are two points to keep in mind with incremental goals. First, the increment by which you advance your goals will probably become smaller as your performance rises. Second, in setting incremental goals you may need to think about setting your goals differently, rather than continuously striving to complete more of the same. You do not have to ride each session in exactly the same manner each time. You can still look for incremental changes whilst you experiment with sessions that feature a slow or a fast start, or where you build progressively to a fast finish. Incremental training with your power meter helps you progress, but to keep finding increments you will have to work increasingly hard and accept smaller gains.

TRAINING GOAL DEADLINES

Your training goal must have a clear deadline. You have to know from the outset when you intend to achieve your goal. Keep in mind that the process of goal setting is about stimulating your focus and motivation. If there is no obvious deadline for you to train towards, then create or invent one. If you really cannot put a time basis to your goal, stop and start again with a new goal

where you can. Remember that nothing beats a deadline in helping ensure that a job gets done!

LONG- AND SHORT-TERM GOALS

One of the ways in which you can help manage your incremental goals is by adopting both short- and long-term goals. The most important of these are your long-term goals. These need to be identified first as they form the fundamental pillars of your training programme. When you start writing your training programme you can break some of your long-term goals into smaller, more manageable chunks by creating short-term goals. In this way each time you achieve one of your short-term goals you move yourself a step closer to your long-term goal.

For example, perhaps your long-term goal is to average 200W for a one-hour training session. Currently, you are capable of training at 175W for one hour, and you can hold 200W for thirty-five minutes. From this several different short-term goals could be created. Taking your current one-hour training session average of 175W, you could set goals that increment from this week-by-week until you reach 200W. Alternatively you set short-term goals for how long you train at 200W, starting from thirty-five minutes and extending this. Finally, you could set short-term goals based around interval training at 200W and increasing the number of intervals you complete. In all these examples, as you achieve each short-term goal you also move closer to achieving your long-term goal.

Before moving on to planning you should write down your goals. Write them somewhere you can see regularly or easily, such as a sticky note on the fridge door, in your diary or in a spreadsheet on the desktop

Performing well in an event relies upon how well you have prepared, and how well you execute your strategy on the day.

SMART GOALS

If you are already familiar with goal setting you may be wondering if I am going to mention SMART goals. This acronym is used to set goals that are:

Specific – Measurable – Achievable – Relevant – Time-based

Other variants of the acronym include goals that are adjustable, realistic and timely.

The problem with SMART goals is that the most crucial aspects of goal setting are not embraced. These crucial aspects form the central tenets of my simple rule of setting incremental training goals with a deadline. Nonetheless, it is worth briefly reviewing SMART goal characteristics, as there is much that is inherently sensible about them.

Specific: A good goal must be specific, clear and unambiguous. It should be set out so that there can be no doubt about what is entailed and how it can be achieved. If it is not specific or leaves room for ambiguity then it is not a goal. It is as simple as that. Riders have often struggled to identify goals that meet this criterion. My rule addresses this problem by guiding you to set specific training goals from the outset.

Measurable: The point of a useful goal is that you should be able to tell if you are on track to achieve it. If your goal is not measurable then the chances are that you will not be able to track your progress towards it. Worse still, if your goal is not easily measurable you risk not being able to tell when or if you achieve it. Discard your goal if it is not quantifiable objectively by someone else. My rule states that you are looking for an incremental improvement, which

immediately helps ensure your goal is measurable.

Achievable: There is a lot of misinformation written about this characteristic. It is obvious that if you do not think your goal is achievable it will not be motivating. But a goal that you know you can achieve is not a useful goal. Can you be optimally focused and motivated to do something you already know is possible? A good goal is one that stretches you, your ability and your resources to the limit. It encourages you to commit fully to achieving something beyond your initial capabilities. Such a goal cannot be safely or comfortably within your reach, nor can you be confident it is achievable from the outset. Research findings are very clear on this point: the more difficult your goal, the higher your performance. If you want to perform at your best you have to pursue the highest goal you can believe is possible. A better word instead of 'achievable' is 'believable'. I know it ruins the acronym. My rule requires you to increment your goals, making them simultaneously believable and challenging.

Relevant: Your goal has to be important to you and what you want to achieve. The outcome has to be worth your effort. My rule in specifying you set training goals helps ensure that they are going to be relevant.

Time-based: Everyone appreciates the drive provided by working to a schedule and the pressure of trying to meet a deadline. That is why it is a central part of my rule. Just be realistic in setting your deadline and resolute in keeping to it.

of your computer. Writing out your goals is a vital part of the process of focusing on what you want to achieve. There are several studies that show writing out your goals in this way increases your likelihood of achieving them.

Planning training

Your training plan is the central part of your overall training strategy. Its main purpose is to convert your goals into action that will help you achieve the goals you have identified. Some riders can find this stage a little daunting but there is no reason too. It is like writing a recipe for baking a cake: you need the list of ingredients and a clear idea of the cake you aim to produce. Here you and your training time are the main ingredients. The cake is the training goals you have set. Your training programme, the recipe, just needs to be formed one step at a time.

Before starting to write your training programme take a moment to think about your current fitness. Your current strengths and weaknesses form the starting point for your training programme, whilst the goals you have set provide your end point. Between the start and finish points is the training you need to complete to achieve your goals. You do not have to make this initial assessment of your current position a complicated or particularly technical process; a simple broad and blunt assessment of your cycling strengths and weaknesses will suffice. If you are already quite fit and competitive you may decide to work on quite specific aspects of your fitness, like your climbing or your sprinting. If your fitness is lower you may first need to build your general fitness in order to be able to

ride further and faster. The main purpose of this initial assessment is to identify how far away you are from achieving your goals. If you are able to quantify the difference between your current fitness and your goal this will of course help you be that much more precise in setting your training programme.

As well as considering your current fitness you also need to take account of the time you have available to train. This ensures that you tailor your programme to match the time you have available. There is no point planning a programme with daily split sessions if you do not have time to train more than once a day. You just need to make a note of which days and for how long you have time to train. A lack of time is often the main reason riders give for not being able to complete their training. With a little forethought at this stage it need not be a factor unless your situation changes.

You should also think about whether there are other things that might act as a barrier to you completing your training successfully. Remember that training is about more than just riding your bike. A diverse range of factors, such as diet, sleep, family commitments, finances, work pressures and other life stresses, will affect your training. If you already have a lot going on in your life, can you manage your cycling goals too? Once you are clear that you have the time and resources to commit to pursuing your cycling goals, then you can start writing your training programme.

As you start writing your training programme decide how you are going to record it. A notebook or diary is ideal as it is good practice to keep a record of your completed training. If you prefer your programme in an electronic format use a word processor or spreadsheet. I prefer the latter as I also use the spreadsheet for training calculations, and I find it easier to update with details of actual sessions as they occur and to amend things as plans change. To begin writing your training programme, look at your goals alongside your strengths and weaknesses. You should already have noted down the aspects of your fitness that you plan to develop and the goals you are going to work towards. Resist the temptation to set lots of goals. You do not need to list many; two to four is about right. These will become the primary focus of your training programme that you are writing.

Assemble your programme using the Training Intensity Bands (TIBs) that I describe in Chapter 5. For each TIB you can identify different kinds of training session to develop the aspects of your fitness you have just listed. For example, you may decide you need a programme that focuses on long TIB2 moderate-intensity endurance sessions. Alternatively, you may feel that an emphasis on high-quality, high-intensity sessions represents the best use of your training time in order to reach your goals.

This stage is about the art of planning and being creative. It cannot be a scientific process as there is insufficient evidence for you to draw upon to write your programme. This is why it is important to experiment with what training works for you, and to be prepared to change your programme if you do not think you are progressing. Try to identify or create one or more training sessions for each fitness aspect. Your aim is to create a short list of target training sessions that you can then use to assemble a day-by-day training programme. If the deadline for your goal is more than four or five weeks away, break your training programme into shorter periods. This means you do not plan all your training at once but rather construct your programme in blocks of between one and four weeks. Writing your programme in short training blocks helps you to make modifications easily. You can alter a few training sessions in one block without having to rewrite your whole programme.

At this point I often find it helpful to work backwards from your ultimate goal. First write down how you would like to train in the last few days before the event. In this way you can create the perfect approach to your ultimate goal. Then think broadly about each of the preceding training blocks. For each of your blocks, set out its aims and the aspects of your performance you aim to improve.

Your final step is to create a varied training programme for each block. You construct each training block by combining the time slots you have available to train with the selection of target sessions from your list. In doing this try and create a varied programme, so mix up the sequence of your different sessions. Depending upon how much time you have available for training, this process may be straightforward. If you have a lot of time to train you will need to decide when to train and when to allow yourself more recovery. There is no easy way of deciding this. If you do not have much experience, err on the side of caution initially. Also keep your training blocks short, for example no more than two or three weeks long, and experiment with different training combinations block by block.

Once complete, your training programme should set out step by step how you will achieve your goals. Keep it somewhere readily accessible as it will act a little like a contract. It will encourage you to train even when you do not feel like it or are struggling

PLANNING TRAINING VERSUS A TRAINING PROGRAMME

There is a difference between planning your training and your training programme itself. Planning is the process that leads to the production of your training programme. The process of planning your training starts with setting goals and finishes with the evaluation of your training. Your training programme is obviously a critical outcome from the planning process.

One way of envisaging the difference between your training planning and your training programme is to consider training without planning. Without planning, you could simply download a programme from a website or borrow someone else's. Whilst the programme you obtain in this way may be fine, it may not be appropriate for your goals. A programme acquired without planning may not reflect your fitness nor fit the time and resources you have for training, and ultimately if it does not work there is little point in refining a programme written for someone else.

to find the time. It should also help hold you back when you are feeling strong and tempted to ride harder or longer than you planned. Riders can rue the session where on the spur of the moment they deviated from their plan because they felt good. With your training programme in place you are ready to move on to the last stage of your training strategy. After all, to monitor and evaluate your training you must have a programme in the first place.

Monitor, evaluate and develop your plan

It is not possible to produce the right training programme precisely. Cycling and training are too complicated. Even if it were possible to know the ideal combination of sessions for maximum training benefit, there is still the challenge of perfectly anticipating what will happen in your future. You might produce a perfect training programme only to find circumstances in your day-to-day life conspiring against you. Consequently, do not think of your plan as immutable, like a fixed contract for your training success, as it will fail at some point. The antidote for this fixed mindset is to set out from the beginning to monitor, evaluate and develop your training plan. Embracing changes in this way from the outset means you can regularly seek to improve and adjust your training programme. This enables your plan to evolve and develop for the better.

MONITOR

Monitoring your training programme is straightforward: you double-check whether your training is following what is written in your programme. It does not take long but it's important that you do this carefully. You are looking to identify the discrepancies between your plan and your actual training. As you check your programme against what you have completed, ask yourself the following questions.

It's important from the beginning to monitor, evaluate and develop your training plan.

- Did you train longer or shorter than the planned time or distance, and if so by how much?
- Was your training intensity or average power output higher or lower than expected?
- Did you perform the planned number of repetitions?

In my experience, surprisingly few riders and coaches ever do this. Often it is just assumed that a training session was completed as intended without ever checking. Professor Carl Foster, a leading sports scientist from Wisconsin, decided to study this. He compared the training actually completed by fifteen athletes with the programme designed by their coaches. Professor Foster found significant differences between the coaches' intended and the athletes' actual training loads. Worse still. Professor Foster found an obvious bias in how athletes trained. When the prescribed session was low intensity, the athletes trained too hard. Conversely when the coaches specified a high-intensity session the athletes trained too easily. The athletes did this without changing the length of their training sessions. Therefore a cursory inspection of their training log would suggest that the athletes had trained as intended.

Professor Foster concluded in his study that athletes might be able to improve their training just by following their programme more carefully. Training with a power meter makes it simple to establish if your intended and actual training loads match. Most software and websites will present your power meter data in a manner that makes it easy to look at the time spent in each of your TIBs. From this you can quickly determine whether this is consistent with your training programme.

EVALUATE

Evaluating your training is going a step further than monitoring your training data. Evaluation means looking for patterns in the data you have been monitoring. In your power meter data you are looking for evidence that your training is progressing as expected. If you are training effectively over a sufficient period of time you should be able to detect signs that your fitness has improved. Evaluating your training simply involves looking for these signs.

Obvious examples that you are progressing are an increase in your training speed or power output. If you regularly ride particular routes look to see if your average power output for the route is creeping up. Over different training roads see if you can spot where you have achieved the same average power output for a longer ride. Websites such as Strava and Map My Tracks which allow you to monitor training segments are particularly useful for this. Upload your data after your ride and the website will automatically find the segments you have ridden before and rank your performances. You should find that changes in these become visible after just a few weeks of training.

Over a longer time period of weeks and months you should be able to see signs that your body has adapted to your training too. Although this is slightly more sophisticated, you are looking for signs that your power output is higher for a given heart rate. The best way of looking for this is to note your average heart rate for a whole ride and your corresponding power output. Do not look within a single ride as your power output and heart rate vary too much to be used easily and reliably. Find rides you have recorded that are both of a similar length and a average heart rate, then compare your average power output. If your fitness has improved notably you should find that your power output has increased.

From these examples you will note that the important changes you are looking for are reflected in the quality or intensity of your training. You can also look to see whether there are changes in the amount of training you are completing, but in general such changes tend to be less important. Conducting these evaluations may involve a little more effort than monitoring your training, but the information gained from your evaluation can have a profound impact on the success of your training programme.

DEVELOP AND CHANGE YOUR PLAN
Having taken the time to monitor and evaluate your programme, it is important that you act on the lessons learnt from the process. The reality is that changing your behaviour, even when it's your own training, is not always as easy as you think. You may find that you are either reluctant to change, or that having made a change you slide back into your old training habits. If you find this happening remind yourself that you are changing your programme to get more benefit from it. Remember too that you are making the changes after learning from what you have done and out of a desire to improve further.

To facilitate making regular changes, it is useful to write your programme in short training blocks. These blocks of training programme set out what you will do for just a few weeks, rather than several months at a time. The transition between training blocks is a natural point for you to evaluate and introduce change. At the end of each training block, review how your training has gone. If things have not gone so well,

try to identify where change is necessary and modify your next programme block. Structuring your training in this way is also consistent with the findings of some of the most recent research, as training structured in blocks has been found to be more effective.

Often you will find that you are unsure about what has worked and what has not in your programme. You will have to decide on a hunch or intuition what to keep and what to change. You should view change in your training as the norm rather than the exception, though. It is rare for training to run perfectly, even for elite athletes in their final build up to a major competition such as the Olympic Games. It is common for elite riders to make changes to their training programme and sometimes their ability to train at all can be compromised. Riders I know have competed successfully after root canal work, major abdominal surgery, serious back injury and even a broken leg! The point here is not the injury but that it could not have been planned for. Clearly under these extreme circumstances the riders' plans have to change. Yet they were still able to win, and in three of these four examples the riders went on to become World or Olympic champions.

Sometimes it even seems possible that these incidents catalyse changes that help performance. Dr Tom Stafford is a psychologist who studied more than 850,000 people learning a new skill. He picked out the people who showed excellent long-term progression and compared them with people who did not improve so well. What he found was that the skilled performers seemed to experiment and try to change things in order to find ways to improve. Those who showed much lower rates of improvement also varied their practice

less. Put another way, it seems obvious that training the same way will lead to the same performance. So it follows that adjusting or changing your plan is necessary to improve your performance. This is particularly true where your evaluation flags that your training is not progressing as you intended.

GET A COACH

There is a lot more to training with a power meter than can be covered in this book alone. Some aspects of training with your power meter may not seem simple. If you are focused on improving your cycling ability then you might benefit from the more personalized guidance provided by a coach. A good coach can help you with everything from identifying and setting your goals appropriately to analysing your power meter data after your ride and checking that you are progressing according to plan.

Oliver Rodriguez during the individual chronometer at the 2002 Giro d'Italia. (Isantilli/Shutterstock.com)

CHAPTER FOUR

PRINCIPLES OF TRAINING WITH POWER METERS

The principles of training provide a useful scheme for thinking about how training with a power meter works. Whilst there is evidence to support the principles, do not regard them like laws of physics. There is still a lot that is not known or cannot be explained fully by these training principles.

The core principles of training are overcompensation, overload, recovery, progression, reversibility and specificity. I will discuss each of these in turn in this chapter. Sometimes these principles are described slightly differently by other people, but the foundations are usually very similar.

OVER-COMPENSATION

Overcompensation is also sometimes called 'supercompensation'. It is the principle of overcompensation that governs the improvement in fitness you achieve as a result of training.

In Figure I you can see a schematic diagram of the overcompensation or training model. You can think of the green lines as representing how your fitness changes with training and recovery. If you imagine that your power meter could plot what was happening to your fitness as you trained and then recovered afterwards, the pattern shown in Figure I is roughly what it would show you. First it would show your fitness falling during your training session as you gradually become fatigued. Then after you finish training and begin recovery it would show your fitness being restored. Notice in Figure I that your fitness does not recover to where you started. Instead you recover to a higher level than before. This elevation in fitness is your training overcompensation. You train, recover, and your body adapts by overcompensating. If your body did not overcompensate like this you would not get fitter. Instead after each training session your body would simply recover to the same level from which you started and you would not adapt. Thus, adaptation is a key part of the overcompensation model and hence your training process. Adaptation is your body's ability to change in response to the stress or stimulus that your training sessions cause. For the most part you can think of adaptation and overcompensation as synonymous in the context of your training.

The process of adaptation and overcompensation happens because your training is stressful. The consequence of overcom-

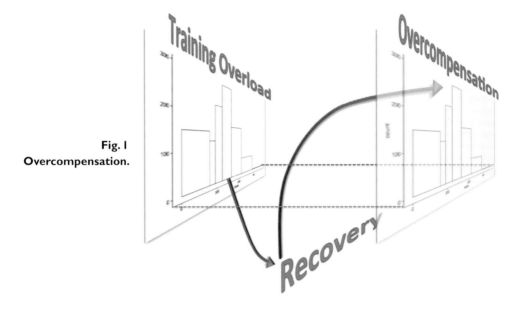

**Fig. I
Overcompensation.**

pensating is that the next time you ride your bike (or race) your body is better prepared to cope with the stress your training imposes. Your body has adapted. Training is the process of causing your body to adapt and making the most of the resulting overcompensation. When you train repeatedly you are trying to overcompensate repeatedly to accumulate lots of adaptation and improve your performance. An increase in your muscle size is a simple example of this principle at work. You may not notice it immediately as it can take many sessions before the extent of overcompensation becomes obvious.

Training effectively is about maximizing the effect of your overcompensation. You are also striving to use the minimum training possible to acquire the maximum adaptation. This should always be the key objective for you in your training programme. Training with a power meter enables you to measure the effects of overcompensation in your power output. When you train

with your power meter and a heart rate monitor you may notice that your training adaptations result in your power output being higher for a given heart rate. That increase in power output is a measure of the overcompensation you have achieved through training.

OVERLOAD

The process of overcompensation starts with a training overload. If you do not apply a sufficient overload to your body during training you will not get any fitter. Assuming you are sitting quietly as your read this book, it is unlikely that you are working hard enough to get fitter. You need to stress your body in order to provide a stimulus for it to adapt and overcompensate. Once you finish reading you might get out your bike and hit the road (perhaps inspired to apply some of the things in this book). From a training principles perspective, the decision that you now have to make is at what power output you should ride. Sitting reading quietly was not a sufficient overload but is an easy spin enough, or perhaps you should go all out in uphill sprints?

When you are training with your power meter you have to think about what constitutes an appropriate training overload. Without an overload your body has no cause to adapt and you will not get fitter. If your power output in training does not provide a sufficient overload for your body, you are almost certainly not making best use of your time and you risk not getting fitter. (The exception to this is of course recovery rides and I'll return to this point later.) Clearly, the exact nature of your training overload is something that merits careful consideration. Fortunately by training with a power meter you are able to use it to apply the lessons of others to your own training. Better still, your power meter is the prime tool for measuring and monitoring your training overload. How you do this will be the focus of Chapter 5 where I discuss the use of Training Intensity Bands (TIBs).

If you look again at the overload in Figure 1, it arises from the entire training session. During this time the line indicating your fitness declines. This is because your training causes fatigue and so is a destructive process. A training overload is required as a stimulus to improve your fitness, but this overload initially reduces your performance and does not increase it. This is a simple yet important point and one that many riders (including me as a young rider) fail to absorb and appreciate. If you are unsure about this, imagine that you have to produce your best effort on your bike. You are allowed to choose to do this either at the beginning of a very hard training session or the

end. Which would you choose? Of course you would choose the beginning. As you proceed through your training session you will progressively fatigue from your training overload and feel increasingly tired. The consequence of your fatigue and tiredness is that your performance also declines. How you balance the necessary but destructive effect of your training overload with your recovery is key to training effectively. So let us now move on to examine the principle of recovery further.

RECOVERY

Once you finish your training session your recovery begins. During your recovery your fitness is restored. Because of this, and perhaps contrary to what I suggested before, you may therefore be getting fitter as you sit reading this book. This would be happening if you are still recovering from a recent training session, not from applying an overload in training. The key point to remember about your recovery is that this is when you accrue the benefits of your training. Your training overload is destructive but stimulates your body to adapt. This adaption is what improves your fitness and it occurs during your recovery. Clearly you do not want to skimp on this most critical aspect of your training process.

Recovery is perhaps the most challenging training aspect to manage well. The difficult thing about recovery is determining how much you need. Your recovery does not follow a set time course. Measuring recovery after training has been the subject of considerable research effort by sports scientists for many years. Although many approaches have been studied (such as your hormone balance and the variability of your

Without an overload your body has no cause to adapt and you will not get fitter.

Elite riders will sometimes use races as part of their training programme.

heart rate), no definitive solutions have been found. Therefore your best guide to recovery remains how you feel.

Although there are twenty-four hours in a day, do not fall into the trap of assuming your body will recover over a similar time course. Training with a set pattern, such as every day or every other day, does not guarantee your level of recovery, although a lot of riders train as if it does. Figure 2 depicts what happens if you train regularly with insufficient recovery. Instead of promoting a positive training adaptation and finding your fitness increase, the opposite happens. Following each session recovery is incomplete and your fitness is not fully restored before the next training session begins. After several training sessions with incomplete recovery, your fatigue has increased progressively and you will be unable to train effectively.

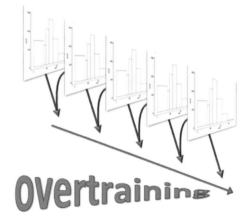

Fig. 2 Overtraining.

Training with your power meter can help you better manage and understand your recovery needs. You can use it to set limits on your power output when you are on a recovery ride. And when your recovery has been insufficient, training with your power meter will enable you to spot quickly that a work rate you usually perceive as moderate now feels hard to achieve. This can be an important sign that you should change your training plan for that session or perhaps not even train at all.

Sometimes you may deliberately plan to push on in your training programme and train even when you are tired. The idea behind doing this is that you can achieve a bigger training overload by limiting your recovery time. Elite riders will sometimes use races, especially stage races, as part of their training programme for the same reason. It has to be said, though, that racing yourself fit in this way is becoming regarded as a rather old-fashioned approach. When you are racing you are not in control of your overload or recovery, and the additional fatigue can easily overwhelm any positive benefits from the greater training stimulus over a period of time. Scientists

are interested in whether you get a larger adaption when you eventually fully recover from this harder-than-usual training period. Figure 3 provides a schematic diagram of a heavy training period. Currently, though, the scientists' findings are equivocal. What does seem to be clear is that training at lower work rates because you are already tired is not helpful.

As your fitness improves you should find that your recovery rate also improves. Thus what might once have been a demanding session can become a routine session, one from which you bounce back rapidly. This brings us to the principle of progression.

PROGRESSION

The principle of progression is shown in Figure 4. Your aim is to ensure that your fitness shows progression with regular increases. However, as your fitness changes

Fig. 3 Heavy training.

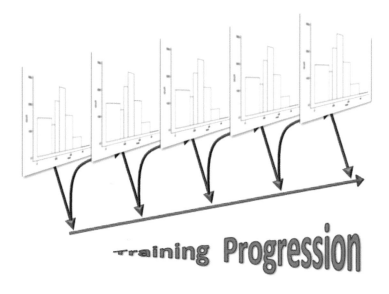

**Fig. 4
Progression.**

training Progression

with training you will need to compensate by altering the nature of your overload and recovery. The principle of progression means that you need to keep changing your training if you want to continue improving. Initially, your training sessions may represent a sufficient overload to cause your body to adapt and overcompensate. But at some point these repeated training sessions become familiar and less stressful. Once this happens your body will no longer need to adapt and you will find your training is causing you to maintain rather than gain fitness.

Any increases in fitness brought about by overcompensation need to be reflected by progression in your training overload too. If you repeat the same training sessions in the same way, you cannot have progression in your programme, or your fitness. The key is to ensure that you regularly increment the overload in your training plan. This will increase the demands your training sessions impose upon you and continue your progression.

Training with your power meter makes

introducing and quantifying your progression straightforward. By training with your power meter you can target a set power output for a session, training segment or interval. By working to a given power output your training is not unduly influenced by day-to-day changes in gradient, wind or temperature. This gives you the opportunity to try and dictate your training progression with precision. Imposing progression on your training like this can quickly become very demanding. Remember that progression means repeatedly asking more of yourself. Training with a power meter means an accurate measurement of your work rate is always right in front of you on your handlebars. However, pushing yourself this way in training is probably a critical element in reaching demanding goals. Training with a power meter offers no scope for slacking and plenty of opportunity for disillusionment if you cannot sustain the progression you seek. It can be a difficult balance to achieve and a reason why some riders do not always enjoy training with a power meter. Equally, being able to set yourself targets to achieve in this manner can, when managed carefully, prove very motivating and highly effective too.

REVERSIBILITY

I doubt you need me to explain the principle of reversibility at length. You are doubtless aware of how your fitness deteriorates when you don't train for a sufficient period of time. This is the principle of reversibility at play. It is where all the benefits of those demanding training sessions you have completed begin to disappear. As with recovery, there are no hard-and-fast rules for the time period over which this will start to happen. Train too much or allow yourself insufficient recovery, and your fitness will suffer through overtraining. But if you do not train with adequate frequency, intensity and duration your fitness will also dissipate, only for a completely different reason. Successful training requires you to achieve a delicate balancing act of opposing factors.

My experience is that training and the reversibility principle work a little like using a dynamo to maintain a rechargeable battery. At the extremes there are two strategies for keeping the rechargeable battery charged: you can either charge it fully at every opportunity, or you can try and ensure that it has enough power for its next use. Those riders who train long and hard combat reversibility in a way that is equivalent to cranking the dynamo regularly to keep the battery fully charged. If they stop training, or charging the battery, it takes some time before the reversibility effects kick in and the battery goes flat. In contrast, those riders who focus on quality rather than quantity in their training are equivalent to using the dynamo to provide the battery with sufficient charge for its next use. Stopping training under this regime quickly reveals the effects of reversibility or a dead battery. The trade-off here is that those who train long and hard are not necessarily any faster, so they train longer to race at the same speed but feel the effects of reversibility less acutely if they have to stop or reduce training. Note that this is not a recommendation to train one way or another. It is based on experience rather than scientific evidence. If I thought you should adopt a particular approach I would tell you.

There is some indirect evidence that the pull that reversibility exerts gets stronger the fitter you are. This is not a core aspect of the principle but it seems likely, and has two obvious implications. First, you will find it much easier to make your initial training gains whilst your fitness is still relatively low. As your fitness increases, so too does the pull of reversibility. For this reason, you will probably have to work considerably harder to make the same gains as those that came easily early on. The second implication is for when you stop training. The speed with which your fitness 'reverses' is greater the higher your fitness. There are both physiological (de-training) and statistical (regression to the mean) reasons for this effect. One of the most eminent sports scientists, Professor Bengt Saltin, conducted a classic study in which he asked his participants to remain in bed. At the end of the study the fitness tests revealed that those who started with a lower level lost notably less than the super-fit participants. Therefore a few days training after Christmas may get you right back to where you were, but the effects of an enforced rest when you are going well mid-season may be all too apparent for a while afterwards.

SPECIFICITY

Specificity is one of the most remarkable and yet obvious aspects of the way our bodies respond to training. The principle of specificity simply tells us that the responses and adaptations you get are specific to the training you have done. Ride your bike and you get fitter at cycling, but you do not necessarily get the same benefits for other activities. Therefore, having improved considerably on your bike after a period of training, the principle of specificity dictates that you will not necessarily experience the same benefit when you then run or swim. That's because the adaptations you have obtained are specific to cycling.

This can have some important implications for the challenges you set yourself, especially if you are cycling to improve your fitness generally. The principle of specificity raises the question of 'fit for what?' Are you training to improve in a range of different activities or is your focus a cycling-specific one? Of course you will benefit from a small crossover of fitness between different activities. A good endurance athlete for example is likely to perform better than average in a range of different but similar sports. But consider triathlon where triathletes have to train in all three disciplines. Because of the specificity principle, they cannot rely on their cycling training to keep them fit for running.

There is another very important aspect of specificity that is sometimes overlooked when this principle is discussed. This aspect of specificity is not just about whether you run or cycle, but about how you cycle. If you always conduct your training in a particular way your strengths and weaknesses will reflect this. Train only at high intensities or at low cadences, for example, and your fitness will reflect this. For example, it has become popular to advocate high-intensity training as a more time efficient way of getting fit. Now there is clear evidence that high-intensity training does work in a time-efficient manner. But the specificity principle causes us to ask again, 'fit for what?' Most of the studies that have examined high-intensity training typically assess its effects with a high-intensity fitness test. It is perhaps unsurprising then that high-intensity training is found to be effective at improving this type of fitness. It is much less clear what high-intensity training does for your endurance fitness, especially as the endurance cycling tests used in a laboratory typically last only an hour. In contrast, out on the road many riders would not even bother getting changed if they had only an hour in which to train. For rides lasting several hours, the specificity of short high-intensity training remain to be determined.

Cross Training

Cross training is a popular activity for many riders, especially during the off-season. The importance of the principle of specificity needs to be considered carefully in this context. The rationale behind cross training may be thought of in two different ways. One rationale is that cross training provides a supplementary training method for getting fit, i.e. perhaps doing some running or swimming instead of cycling. The other rationale for cross training is to target those aspects of your fitness that are difficult to achieve by cycling alone. Weight training and stretching are examples of exercises that you might deliberately perform off the bike, in order to develop specific cycling fitness. Although the distinction between these two rationales may seem subtle, only one of these is a good idea if you are serious about improving your on the bike performance. Hopefully from the preceding discussion on specificity, you may be able to spot that cross training as a supplementary training method is unlikely to be particularly effective. If you want to get fit for riding a bike, ride a bike! If riding a bike is not an option, then by all means do something else instead. But do not deliberately substitute an alternative form of training for cycling in the mistaken belief that it will make you a better bike rider. This contravenes the principle of specificity.

The situation in which you can make specificity work for you is when you are training off the bike to improve a very particular aspect of your cycling fitness. Let us consider your leg strength as an example. If you want to improve your leg strength, most coaches and sports scientists agree that to do this you should try to create very high forces in your leg muscles. However, when cycling it can be very difficult to generate forces that are much in excess of your body weight. Therefore to really overload your leg muscles and improve your strength by generating high forces, it makes sense to go to the gym and work with a coach there. By weight training in the gym you can create much higher forces than are normally possible on your bike. Similarly, if you want to improve your flexibility or your upper body strength and core fitness, it may be much better to perform the necessary exercises off your bike. Consequently, when planning cross training you should think very carefully about how the principle of training specificity can be used to target the particular improvements you are seeking.

There is one further point on cross training that I would like to make clear. I have been critical of the benefits of some non-cycling training as a means of improving your cycling

specific fitness. But please do not interpret this as a reason not to include off the bike training in your programme. There are many reasons for completing a range of different types of training that may not directly result in you being able to ride faster. Injury prevention, posture correction, all-round fitness, and physical literacy are just some examples. These are particularly important for younger and older riders as both groups may obtain great benefit from a wider programme than cycling alone can provide. Just be clear on why you are engaged in a cross training session and whether it is focused on enabling you to cycle faster.

A FINAL POINT ON PRINCIPLES OF TRAINING

These 'principles' of training should be seen as general philosophies and ideologies providing useful guidelines, rather than as hard-and-fast rules or laws. For each of the training principles above you may come across situations which they cannot explain or where they do not apply. For example, in my research I regularly look at training data from power meters in order to find clues on how to train more effectively. One of the striking things about analysing riders' power-meter training data is how much it can vary. These variations can be very noticeable from rider to rider but also from ride to ride with the same rider, and on occasion even within the same ride. My research suggests that these variations may be important for training effectively. But in terms of the principles discussed here the reason for this cannot easily be explained. Analysis of training with power meters at this level is really the topic for a different book altogether!

TRAINING
INTENSITY BANDS

INTRODUCTION TO TIBs

Chapter 4 highlighted the importance of quantifying your training overload. Power meters are excellent tools for achieving this, but they also risk making training planning and analysis complicated. Fortunately for most training purposes this complexity is neither necessary nor justified. Instead you can simplify the process of training with your power meter by adopting Training Intensity Bands (TIBs). The main point of TIBs is to keep the process of describing and quantifying training with a power meter as simple and jargon-free as possible. The key to using your power meter successfully revolves around hard training and a sensible strategy to plan and evaluate what you do.

I have based the TIBs system on more than twenty-five years' experience of working in elite cycling. During this time I have presented and published many research papers on training and performance. There is some complexity within the TIBs system but I have tried to keep this largely invisible. You may notice that TIBs are calculated slightly differently from other power-meter zone systems in order to make them even easier to use.

The important principle of applying a training overload was identified in the previous chapter. Finding the best way of achieving a training overload is something that has preoccupied riders, coaches and scientists for many years. TIBs provide a simple way of quantifying the training session overload. Adopting TIBs also allows you to explore how overload interacts with the other training principles such as recovery, specificity or progression.

When you plan, monitor and evaluate your training, the process can quickly get rather complicated. Using TIBs helps keep this process simple by categorizing all your training into a TIB based on your training intensity. There are several benefits to chunking your training into bands, but the main one is that your training overload is much easier to consider and manage when expressed in this way. Do consider your TIBs a training tool and, like a good craftsman, be prepared to experiment with how best to use them.

ORGANIZATION OF TIBs

The way TIBs are organized is shown schematically in Figure 5 and a brief summary

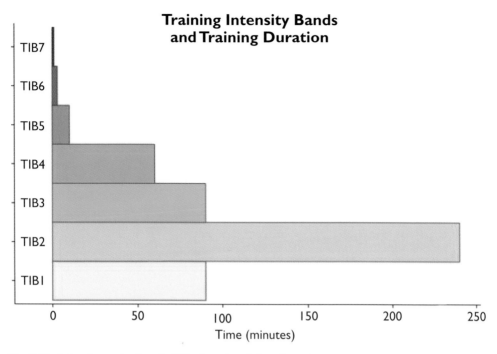

Fig. 5 Training intensity bands (TIBs) and training duration.

of each TIB is shown in Table 2. Your train-ing intensity is categorized into one of seven different TIBs. You can see that the seven TIBs are numbered sequentially: TIB1, TIB2, TIB3, TIB4, TIB5, TIB6 and TIB7. The lowest or easiest TIB (TIB1) is a non-training or recovery TIB. The highest inten-sity or hardest TIB is for highly structured, short-interval training sessions consisting of maximal or near maximal efforts. There-fore TIB1 and TIB7 identify the minimum and maximum possible training intensities respectively.

Each TIB is calculated as a minimum and a maximum power output, and the middle of each TIB is also identified. Your TIBs are individual to you. This is because each TIB provides your relative training intensity and depends on your level of fitness. The fitter you are the higher the power output range

will be for each TIB. When you are starting out you first have to determine the power output for each of your TIBs. This means you must calculate your own TIBs. You cannot 'borrow' someone else's, even if the person is someone you know has a similar level of fitness to you. However, your TIBs are easy to establish. With just one or two tailored training sessions you can establish and start using your own personal TIBs.

I use a total of seven TIBs when train-ing with a power meter but the number of TIBs is not an exact science. Many years ago, when I first started working in sports science with heart rate zones, I used only four quite satisfactorily. In fact in the TIB descriptions provided in Table 2 I have included the maximum heart rate bands only up to TIB4. Beyond TIB4 heart rate is not a reliable measure of intensity and

Table 2. HOW TIBs WORK

Training Intensity Band	Session RPE (at start)	Sensations	Description
TIB1 - Active Recovery *Up to 90 minutes*	1 to 2	Very, very easy, or Easy Breathing easy, rate low Heart rate < 70% maximum	A non-training band used for easy, fun riding and active recovery. Restrict to less than 90 minutes. Alternatively, use TIB for long rides when you are unused to regular cycling, or in preparation for very long events. Use also for recovery between efforts when interval training.
TIB2 - Moderate *Up to several hours*	2 or 3	Easy or Moderate Breathing comfortable, rate fairly light Heart rate 75 to 82% maximum Sweating barely noticeable and light	The lowest intensity that provides a training overload. This is the classic endurance training intensity for steady long and group rides. It is possible to train frequently at this intensity, or to perform long rides of several hours. Longer rides will increase recovery time though.
TIB3 - Tempo *45 to 90 minutes*	3 to 5	Moderate or Somewhat Hard Breathing regular, rate steady Heart rate 82 to 87% Sweating notable, regular drink needed	This is a demanding endurance training intensity. It is typical of sustained hard group riding. Training at this intensity requires you to be motivated and concentrated. If you are an elite rider or looking to improve your road race endurance you can extend rides up to 3 hours.
TIB4 - Race pace *20 to 60 minutes*	5 to 7	Hard to Very Hard Breathing deep and very regular Heart rate 87 to 95% Sweating heavy and fluid loss notable	This is controlled hard, or very hard race pace type training. Sometimes called "threshold" training. Performed as long intervals (> 5 minutes) or as a consistent paced ride or climb. For demanding endurance training you add 5 to 20 minute TIB4 blocks to a longer TIB2 ride.

Training Intensity Band	Session RPE (at start)	Sensations	Description
TIB5 - Intervals *1 to 10 minute efforts*	7 or 8	Very Hard Breathing deep, increasing throughout Heart rate unreliable in short intervals Sweating very heavy in long intervals	These are intervals at a controlled training intensity for efforts lasting several minutes. They boost your ability to power up short climbs. Perform these with short or medium recovery periods. These intense sustained efforts can maximally stress your cardiorespiratory system.
TIB6 - Top end *1 to 3 minutes*	9	Near Maximal Breathing panting by end of effort Heart rate unreliable at this intensity	Very high intensity near maximal efforts lasting only 1 to 3 minutes. These efforts require full commitment and motivation to continue despite the symptoms of marked fatigue. They can feel unpleasant and require a good recovery between each effort or your power output falls.
TIB7 - Sprint *5 to 60 seconds*	10	Maximal Breathing maximal if effort long enough Heart rate unreliable at this intensity	Short maximal efforts lasting only a few seconds. Used to improve your hard accelerations, sprint technique and performance. Use your power meter to record these and report back your maximum power output. Can also be used for repeated sprints but the effect is different.

so is not included. Training with a power meter enables you to measure your training intensity much more accurately than with a heart rate monitor. This is especially true for the high intensity TIBs (TIB5, TIB6 and TIB7) and therefore justifies the creation of these extra bands.

The TIBs are defined in terms of your power output in watts. Each TIB has been designed to accommodate a range around your target power output because you cannot consistently ride to a single power output within a single session. Consequently, your TIBs do not need to be prescribed too tightly. Rather you should try and accumulate training time within your target TIBs. It is your training time in the designated TIB that provides your training overload.

Your TIBs are given numbers rather than names. This is deliberate. These numbered TIBs permit your training sessions to be described unambiguously. Anyone discussing your training is able to adopt the same simple and clear terminology. Using TIB numbers also helps avoid introducing unnecessary jargon. Coaches and athletes often discuss training in terms of strength, power, speed, endurance, speed-endurance, threshold, and so on. These terms may be helpful when discussing the training theory. But when you are translating training theory into practice they are not needed and can complicate simple communication. Worse, as these terms can mean different things to different coaches they can lead to misunderstanding. Of course any misunderstanding detracts from the main purpose of a training programme, which is to precisely describe specific training sessions. For these reasons I have deliberately sought to minimize the amount of training jargon used. In general I prefer to let your TIBs speak for themselves without creating too many additional complicated metrics. If you are familiar with the training data from your power meter you will also understand the meaning of your watts and TIBs. Unless used wisely, additional metrics can confuse rather than clarify the picture of your training.

TRAINING INTENSITY BAND I

The lowest training band, TIB1 starts at 0W and goes up to somewhere between 80W and 200W, depending on your fitness. Training in TIB1 is too easy to be effective for increasing your fitness as it cannot provide a training overload. This TIB is therefore largely for easy, fun and recovery riding. In other words you should regard it as a non-training band.

There are some general exceptions to this non-training guideline that are worth highlighting, however. If you are only just starting out on a training or haven't trained for some considerable time, then you will find some benefit from riding in TIB1 before changing your sessions to include the other TIBs. During high-intensity interval sessions, you will often alternate between very hard efforts and easy recovery periods. During the recovery periods between hard efforts you should ride in TIB1. Similarly, if you are training to develop challenging technical skills, such as when descending or mountain biking, riding in TIB1 initially can be helpful. Later, once you have developed the requisite skills, increase the speed and intensity of your training. Lastly, if the event for which you are preparing is considerably longer than you are used to riding, extending your training duration by starting off riding in TIB1 is a sensible approach. Once you are used to training regularly then you should normally aim to keep your training out of TIB1.

Some riders choose to boost their training volume by including quite a lot of recovery riding in their training programme. They do this by riding in TIB1 for extended periods, particularly on days when they are not sufficiently recovered to train fully. Unless you have a specific reason for doing this, such as those discussed in the previous paragraph, I would caution against this approach. Whilst TIB1 may not be an effective training intensity you can still end up working hard enough to delay your recovery. Increasing the time until you are ready for your next full training session in this manner is not a particularly effective strategy, although limited recovery riding can make you feel better than not training at all and possibly even speed up recovery. However, if you are to benefit from recovery riding I suggest that these rides need not be particularly long and probably an hour is sufficient for all but the most elite riders. The obvious exception to the above and where riding in TIB1 would be sensible is if you are preparing to ride long hours in the saddle over many days. Such consecutive day-after-day riding would be typical of events such as a cycling tour or stage race.

TRAINING INTENSITY BAND 2

Training at TIB2 provides the traditional backbone of your endurance-training programme. The main focus of TIB2 training is to develop both your aerobic and endurance fitness. Both your VO_2max and your ability to metabolize fat should respond to training in TIB2 (and TIB3). This means that you should be able to measure progressive increases in both your training speed and distance from this type of training.

At TIB2 it is perfectly possible to train for several hours. The sensations of training at TIB2 are that you are working in a moderately focused but very sustainable manner. You will be aware that your breathing rate is elevated from rest, but not to such an extent that it interferes with your ability to talk whilst training. The consistent and sustained work rate involved will mean that you sweat lightly. Your perception of effort on the session RPE scale from 0–10 is typically 2 or 3.

Over time, you should find that TIB2 training sessions increase your endurance quite markedly. You will notice this as an increase in how long you can keep going in

RPE

A simple and sensitive way to track changes in your training is to record how hard each session felt overall. In 1970 Professor Gunnar Borg designed a scale to measure the rating of perceived exertion (RPE). Today it is probably one of the best-known measures in sports science laboratories around the world. Professor Borg developed two scales. The first scale ranged from a score of 6 through to 20. He later simplified this by devising a 0 to 10 scale. Subsequent research has established that athletes are surprisingly consistent in how they score

their RPE for a training session. Therefore many scientists and coaches now ask their athletes to record their overall RPE for each training session and it is known as a Session RPE. Your Session RPE is a simple and useful way to record how demanding your training was. Changes in your Session RPE for the same type of training can help indicate changes in fitness and fatigue. Therefore the TIBs are described not only by power output and heart rate but also Session RPE scores from 0-10 and their associated physical sensations.

a TIB2 session. Equally, the power output you can sustain during your TIB2 sessions should show an increase slowly but progressively. Your average speed may show signs of progression too, although of the three aspects mentioned this one may be the hardest to see changes in as so many other factors also influence your speed. As you get fitter, make your TIB2 sessions more challenging by increasing your training duration (in other words, the length of the session). Training over a set distance can be unpredictable as it depends upon the terrain and weather you encounter on your training ride.

Training in TIB2 also provides a good opportunity to develop a smooth, fluid pedalling style. Inexperienced riders often adopt a lower cadence than their more experienced counterparts. Experienced riders will typically pedal comfortably on a long ride at between 80 and 100rpm. With a power meter you can monitor the effects of changing down a gear and pedalling more quickly. With practice you find that you can maintain the same power output whilst pedalling faster. On long rides your higher cadence should have the added benefit of reducing the rate at which you fatigue and your perception of effort increases.

If the event for which you are training will last more than two minutes (or you are building general cycling fitness), the traditional training approach is to build a foundation of fitness by training at TIB2 and TIB3. Training in TIB2 is normally considered the lowest effective training intensity. It is the band that you will train in when on medium- to long-distance or endurance rides. If you are new to TIBs you may initially find it challenging to maintain the required effort. Going up hills, your power output can easily rise out of TIB2. Conversely, as you descend

the other side of the hill it is not always possible to keep a sufficient work rate to prevent yourself dropping below TIB2.

Group riding can also present some challenges, not least because you cannot necessarily dictate the pace of a group of riders. You may find that when you are on the front you are able to push your power output into or beyond TIB2. However, when drafting behind other riders it may not be possible to maintain your desired TIB. For this reason you may prefer to do your serious training rides in a smaller group of similarly committed riders. Alternatively you can split your rides, doing part of it on your own before or after training in company. Of course if you do not have many riders who train nearby, you may have no choice but to ride on your own. But for long training rides typical of TIB2, riding in company can make the process sufficiently more enjoyable and rewarding that it's worth sacrificing a little in terms of the effectiveness of the session. Training with a group also provides you with the opportunity to develop your skill at riding on a wheel. If you plan to race in a bunch it is important that you are used to gaining maximum shelter from other riders when you are not on the front.

TRAINING INTENSITY BAND 3

Riders often refer to TIB3 training as 'tempo training'. It's an upbeat endurance-training intensity. This is definitely not a pace that you would be comfortable with all day. It does not require a race-pace type of concentration or effort either, though. Your TIB3 training sessions are medium-length brisk rides that help build aerobic fitness and some endurance. The duration of your rides normally range between forty-five and ninety minutes. With training, a fit and motivated rider can extend the length of these sessions further but they become very demanding.

Often TIB3 sessions are alternated with longer, steadier TIB2 rides as part of an endurance-building block of training. Sometimes you may even mix TIB2 and TIB3 in the same training session to make a long steady ride that bit more challenging. You need to have good endurance to be able to introduce TIB3 efforts towards the end of a long ride. When training at TIB3 you will be working in a controlled and decidedly focused manner. Your breathing will be regular and, although you can hold a conversation, you will notice your breathing interfering with your speech. On all but the coldest days you will notice that you have been sweating. Indeed, if this intensity of training is introduced into a longer ride you will need to take water bottles with you to drink. During the early part of the session your perception of effort using the session RPE 0–10 scale should be between 3 and 5, or what you perceive to be a moderate to hard effort. However, this rating will increase progressively during your training session.

Training at TIB3 is a classic training intensity adopted by scientists for laboratory-based aerobic and endurance training studies. Moderate-length TIB3 training sessions are very effective in helping you to hold on to your fitness during periods of reduced training. Similarly, you can rebuild endurance fitness quickly with TIB3 if you have had an enforced layoff. For serious competitive riders, longer training rides at TIB3 are both very demanding and potent in building race fitness. Sustained for more than a couple of hours, TIB3 provides an overall stress that is quite similar to a road race.

Broadly speaking, TIB3 can be mixed judiciously with other TIBs to provide a solid aerobic fitness. If you have limited time and are preparing for a challenging sportive, you may well find that regular TIB3 sessions can help you efficiently build the main endurance and aerobic fitness you require. In addition to these regular challenging sessions, you would need to add occasional (weekend) longer and steadier rides to give you the ability to last the distance.

Bear in mind, however, that it has been shown that not everyone responds well to this type of training. Whilst some riders respond rapidly, others find that their fitness does not change at all. It is worth mentioning that elite endurance athletes tend not to include lots of TIB3 (or TIB4) training in their programmes. Generally, they prefer instead to perform longer rides at the lower TIB2 intensity and then 'polarize' their training by riding much more intensely in shorter sessions. A possible reason for preferring this style of polarized training is that longer lower-intensity TIB2 rides and shorter more-intense sessions both require less recovery than demanding TIB3 training (see Chapter 11).

TRAINING INTENSITY BAND 4

Coaches often refer to TIB4 sessions as 'threshold' training. I discuss the concept of a threshold riding pace in Chapter 6. This type of training is similar to sustained race pace, time trial, or long hill- or mountain-climb efforts. The reference to a 'threshold' comes from the sensation that when you are riding this hard a threshold dictates your work rate. Whilst your efforts remain

Training at TIB4 is essential for familiarity with the stresses and strains of racing.

below your threshold you can keep going for quite some time. Once you step over the threshold, very rapidly you begin to fatigue and are forced to stop. (Incidentally, scientists have examined this phenomenon in considerable detail. The consensus is that your sensation of a threshold is not reflected in the underlying physiology or psychology.)

Training at TIB4 is done in medium-length intense bouts typically of around 20 minutes. During TIB4 training you will have to concentrate carefully on the required effort. This type of training will make you breathe heavily and sweat profusely. From the start your perception of effort on the session RPE scale will be 5, 6 or 7. It will rise progressively and approach maximal levels by the end of the training session. Because they are physically and mentally demanding, you will need to be motivated to perform

TIB4 sessions effectively. Nonetheless, if you are in good condition it is possible to recover quite quickly from these training sessions. Consequently, well-trained riders sometimes perform them on split training days, for example in the afternoon following a steady TIB2 ride in the morning. You can also intersperse intervals of TIB4 in longer TIB2 rides. If you try this bear in mind you can significantly reduce the duration of your training ride. Therefore use this combination of intervals judiciously.

Training at TIB4 is essential for familiarity with the stresses and strains of racing. If you are not able or do not wish to compete regularly, use regular TIB4 sessions as part of your event build up. You will also find benefits from TIB4 sessions to prepare for the stress of repeated or extended climbs in a hilly sportive.

Keep in mind too that it also helps to be

as specific as possible with any TIB4 training. Where practicable use the same bike under similar conditions to the event for which you are preparing. For example, if your event is a time trial, train on your time-trial bike in your racing position. If you are an off-road rider training on the road, put road wheels or slicks on your MTB. If your aim is to improve your climbing then perform your TIB4 efforts on a gradient if at all possible. If you live somewhere without long climbs, perhaps you can visit somewhere that you can ride a few hlls at a key point in your preparation? Failing this, ask your local gym or sports science department if they have a treadmill they will let you ride on. A 30 to 45-minute training session on a fixed gradient efficiently simulates a climb that can be otherwise impractical to find.

TRAINING INTENSITY BAND 5

The power output required in TIB5 cannot be sustained for an extended period of time. This means that TIB5 and above has to be performed as short interval-based training bouts. The power output that you need to produce in TIB5 is approximately equal to your power output at a VO_2max test (discussed in Chapter 6). Typically you can sustain this type of effort for between three and six minutes before you fatigue. This means that intervals in TIB5 will be physically demanding. Each effort you make will be very close to maximal by the end. Your perception of effort will be 7 or 8 at the start, quickly rising towards 9 or 10 as you fatigue. The effort of each interval will

If you are a time-triallist or sprint based rider, include TIB5 intervals in your training programme for variety and all-round fitness.

tax both your legs and your heart and lungs. Towards the end of the interval you may find your legs starting to tie up, your heart will be pounding and you will be breathing heavily. After several efforts you will be sweating heavily too.

The fatigue from these efforts is one of its more noticeable effects. Therefore some recovery is necessary between efforts, but you only need sufficient recovery to be able to complete the next effort. Accordingly, intervals in TIB5 need normally have a short- to medium-length recovery. In general, regardless of how you structure intervals you are doing well if you can accumulate thirty minutes or more at TIB5 in one training session. In addition to the more common sustained intervals, try using TIB5 as repeated one-minute intervals with a similar recovery time at TIB1. If this is the first time you have attempted this you could aim to perform ten repetitions at TIB5. Regardless of the number you actually achieve, the next time you repeat the session aim to perform one more than the previous time.

From the above you can appreciate that TIB5 intervals are ideal for maximally stressing your cardiorespiratory system. These kind of stressful efforts help build your ability to sustain high-intensity efforts and resist fatigue. In your typical training you will not often push your body this hard. Therefore controlled, repeated efforts where you nudge your body into this red zone can provide a notable boost to your ability to keep going in the face of increasing fatigue. The kind of fitness that you derive from these intervals is really valuable if your event involves repeated climbs, or if you are road racing or mountain biking. If you are a time triallist or sprint-based rider, include TIB5 intervals in your training programme for variety and all-round fitness.

Due to both the sustained and fatiguing nature of TIB5 interval training you need to pace your efforts carefully. If you start too hard you will find that you are unable to maintain your target power output. Alternatively, you may find that your recovery is insufficient for you to complete the next interval. Training with a power meter particularly helps with these issues. Unlike any other type of device, you can use it to monitor your power output and guide you in pacing your effort. For the next interval start more cautiously and try to hit the power output from the end of the previous interval. As a consequence you should find you are able to gauge your effort more effectively and finish the interval more comfortably. For subsequent intervals you can now try to raise the average by just a few watts. Work at raising your interval average and your end, not starting, power output. Ultimately, your aim is to accumulate as much training time as possible in TIB5. You will achieve this with repeated measured efforts, not by starting fast and trying to hang on as long as possible each time.

TRAINING INTENSITY BAND 6

Working in TIB6 is probably the most nauseating type of effort you can perform on a bike, but do not let that put you off! It can be fun and a potent way of raising the bar on your performance. The power output required for TIB6 means that you will be working at a power output that is well above the maximum power output you can sustain for any reasonable length of time. Like TIB5, pacing these efforts is also quite challenging and important to get right. If you start too hard you simply will not be able to last for the target duration. As with TIB5, your power meter provides by far the best way to monitor your TIB6 efforts. Your heart rate will not provide a useful indication of your effort at this intensity.

Typically your intervals in TIB6 should range between one and three minutes. You need to start each effort hard and with commitment. You will push your power output right to the end of the interval. By the end of the interval your legs will often feel like they are struggling to produce the force required to keep the pedals turning at the same cadence. Your breathing can become quite ragged and you may start to feel a little wobbly on your bike. For these reasons, train in a place where it is safe for you to really exert yourself maximally: on a quiet road, a velodrome or on a static trainer. Resist the temptation to perform *all* your TIB6 intervals on a static trainer, however. This is because producing this kind of power output on your bike is a skill. If you only ever undertake your TIB6 sessions on a static bike you will not develop the associated bike-handling and pedalling skills that enable you to deliver this kind of power on the open road or track.

Because of the intensity of these efforts you will only be able to repeat them if you allow yourself a reasonable-length recovery between repetitions. A minimum of three minutes' recovery between repetitions is common for a TIB6 interval session. If you are really trying to raise your ceiling then even five or six minutes' recovery may not feel sufficient. The physiological stress that these intervals impose is severe, so don't be surprised that even when you allow yourself a reasonable recovery you still feel the progressive accumulation of fatigue from successive repetitions after the first one or two. For this reason this type of

training should normally be performed only when you are feeling fresh and reasonably recovered from previous training sessions. If you try TIB6 when you are tired you simply will not be able to generate or sustain the power output required. The ability to monitor your power output during the interval session and check that you are producing the target power output makes your power meter invaluable in this context.

The benefit of TIB6 training is that it helps raise the ceiling on your fitness. One way to think of this is that TIB2 and TIB3 are effective at improving your fitness by pushing it up from the ground. This approach works fine until you start to bang your head on the ceiling. At this point you need to improve your fitness by raising the ceiling rather than to continue pushing from the floor. In this analogy TIB6 provides the means for raising the ceiling to give you more head space. Teaching your body to produce and sustain the high power outputs associated with TIB6 means that you can appreciate how much easier it is when you ride at TIB2 and TIB3. This in turns gives you confidence to extend yourself in these lower-intensity sessions and nudge your power output up a little. Without these sustained high-intensity TIB6 efforts, it is easy to fall into a trap of believing you are training as hard as possible. But with TIB6 sessions as a reference point you are able to appreciate whether you have more in reserve when you are training in the lower TIBs.

TRAINING INTENSITY BAND 7

Until recent years the diverse benefits of TIB7 training have generally been under-appreciated by riders and coaches. TIB7 is the most intense of your sessions. Training in TIB7 involves you performing maximal or very-near-maximal sprints and accelerations for just a few seconds up to about thirty seconds or a minute in length. Traditionally this kind of TIB7 training has been viewed as a means of increasing your muscle strength and your peak sprinting power output. In recent years, however, several studies have been published that demonstrate that a much wider range of benefits can be derived from training at TIB7. As a consequence TIB7 training (often referred to as High Intensity Training and abbreviated to HIT) has received a lot of attention even in the national media.

Although the duration of intervals in TIB7 covers the range from a few seconds up to one minute, the most commonly used interval-training periods are six seconds, ten seconds and thirty seconds. Intervals in TIB7 are generally performed all-out with little or no pacing. To increase your ability to sprint and accelerate hard, train using short six- to ten-second efforts. During these sessions your aim should be to generate the highest power output possible. Your power meter can be used to record each sprint but, due to the maximal nature of each sprint, you probably will not need or be able to monitor your power output during the sprint itself. Many power meters have a function to recall the maximum power output generated, though, so a quick key press at the end of the sprint is often enough to be able to see how you did. Although these short efforts are exceptionally intense, your symptoms will generally be limited to the fatigue in your legs. This is because TIB7 intervals are not long enough to generate a severe cardiorespiratory response.

Developing sprint or peak power output with TIB7 improves your ability to sprint during or at the end of a race, to surge up small climbs, and to create or bridge gaps with other riders explosively. In road races these kind of manoeuvres often dictate the outcome of key tactical and race-winning moves. Therefore if you are training for road or circuit racing it is important that you include some short TIB7 intervals in your training programme.

The wider interest in using TIB7 that I referred to previously has arisen from the benefits found from training with the longer thirty-second intervals. There have now been many studies, particularly from a Canadian sports science research group, that highlight the effectiveness of using repeated, short, maximal sprints for improving even aerobic fitness. To follow the recommended interval protocol you should try to perform between three and six all-out thirty-second sprints. These sprints are not for the faint-hearted as you perform each interval to your maximum without pacing or measuring your effort in any way. Between each of the sprints you recover and pedal gently for four minutes. However, apart from a warm-up beforehand and a warm down afterwards, that is the whole session: short and tough! But the training session is completed quickly in a time-efficient manner.

The fitness benefit of these short-but-intense sessions has proved to be quite surprising as it extends well beyond enhancing just your sprinting ability. To examine the changes, the Canadian research group conducted a two-week training study. In this training study their participants performed either six sessions of thirty-second TIB7 intervals or six sessions of between one-and-half and two hours of TIB2 constant riding. The TIB7 sessions consisted of four to six repetitions of a thirty-second all-out sprint with four minutes' recovery between each. In total, including recovery time the TIB7 sessions lasted less than half an hour. The scientists measured changes during two different time-trial performances, one lasting about an hour and the other lasting about two minutes.

At the end of the study both TIB2 and TIB7 training groups had significantly improved their performance in both the long and short time trials. Remarkably, the scientists found similar improvements resulting from the distinctly different TIB2 and TIB7 training regimes. The scientists also took small samples of muscle from their participants. This was done in order to compare changes occurring within the muscle from the TIB2 and TIB7 groups. Examined at this microscopic level the effects of training were found clearly, but again these training responses were not different between TIB2 and TIB7 groups.

The conclusions from this study were that sessions involving TIB7 appear to be as effective as TIB2. But of course there were key differences in the amount and intensity of training the two groups had performed. By the end of the study the TIB7 group had completed 90 per cent less training but the work rate sustained during their interval training was four times higher than the TIB2 group. Several other laboratories around the world including my own have gone on to obtain similar findings. Therefore it seems that short TIB7 sessions can provide an effective and efficient training method even for endurance events.

However, a couple of words of caution are merited too. Most studies are very short, typically lasting only a few weeks. It seems quite likely that if they had been able to conduct a longer study the effects of TIB2 and TIB7 may not be so comparable. This is an important distinction as your training programme is likely to last much longer than the studies to date that have compared TIB2 and TIB7.

CHAPTER SIX

AEROBIC AND ENDURANCE FITNESS

Regardless of whether the events you train for are on or off road, a road race, triathlon, time trial or sportive, the vast majority demand good aerobic and endurance fitness. Aerobic or endurance events are those that last from two or three minutes to several hours and beyond. Events lasting two minutes or less become increasingly anaerobic in nature the shorter they are. Although training with a power meter for short anaerobic events is a good idea, the approach to training for this type of fitness is very different and specialist. The use of TIBs is based around training for aerobic and endurance events and not so useful for sprint-based riders. Therefore this book focuses on aerobic and endurance training, although I will discuss sprinting for road races later.

The terms 'aerobic' and 'endurance' are often used interchangeably, although they are not quite the same. Because they are not the same the training principle of specificity means that training for aerobic fitness and endurance can also be somewhat different. The term aerobic relates to the physiology of the body and how it produces energy, in other words aerobically. Endurance simply means activities that last a long time. Therefore good endurance fitness means that you

have the ability to sustain a work rate for a long time. With good endurance fitness you will have the ability to resist both physical and mental fatigue. Conceptually, you could think of your endurance as how long you can keep going at a fixed power output. In practice it is more complicated because your aerobic fitness plays a critical role in determining how long you can ride at a particular power output.

It is because endurance activities depend heavily on aerobic energy production that the two terms are often used synonymously. Aerobic training means training to enhance your body's aerobic system. A very wide range of exercise intensities has been shown to improve aerobic fitness. As discussed at the end of Chapter 5, recent research has highlighted that even short, repeated sprints of around thirty seconds can be effective for increasing aerobic fitness. Endurance training, in contrast, is about developing your ability to resist fatigue and to ride for a long time. Surprisingly, training with short sprints repeated several times has been shown to improve endurance fitness. However, it is unlikely that you will maximize your endurance fitness by training in this way. Instead, to really build your endurance you will have to train by riding for a long time, and

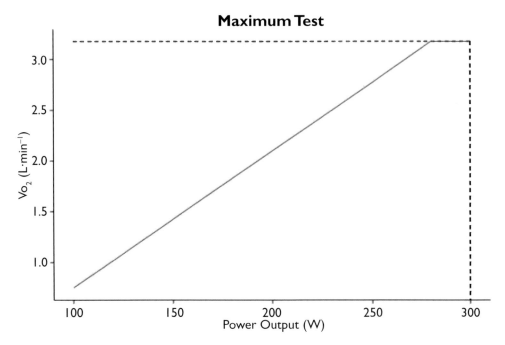

Fig. 6 VO$_2$max test.

to do this you also need to ride at a lower intensity. In this way you will develop your ability to burn fat as a fuel, resist fatigue and cope mentally with the challenge of sustaining prolonged exercise. Nevertheless it is worth remembering when you lack training time that short, repeated sprints can be a useful way of boosting both aerobic and endurance fitness.

MEASURING FITNESS

Because you train to get fitter it is useful to look at what your fitness is and how you measure it. As discussed above, the distinction between aerobic and endurance fitness is subtle. Crudely put, aerobic fitness dictates how fast you can ride for efforts that last longer than a couple of minutes.

Endurance fitness on the other hand determines how long you can keep going on a ride before having to slow down. When you exercise aerobically you do so by consuming oxygen. Your aerobic fitness is dictated by your body's ability to consume oxygen and produce energy aerobically. Therefore the classic scientific way to assess your aerobic fitness is to measure the highest amount of oxygen that you can consume. This measure is called your maximum oxygen consumption and I will refer to it in its scientific form, VO$_2$max. A VO$_2$max test is the equivalent of measuring your engine size if you were a car or a motorbike: the greater your VO$_2$max the larger and more powerful your engine.

The traditional test to measure VO$_2$max is conducted in a laboratory. It requires you to gradually increase your power output, riding harder and harder, until you are unable to keep going. It's like riding up a hill that gets steeper and steeper until you are forced to stop. Typically a VO_2max test lasts about 10 minutes, so it is much more than just a quick sprint. During a VO_2max test you wear a facemask or mouthpiece in order to measure the amount of air you breathe and the oxygen you consume.

Figure 6 shows what happens during a VO_2max test. Your power output is shown along the horizontal axis and the oxygen you have consumed (VO_2) is shown on the vertical axis. You can see at low power outputs your VO_2 is also low; this is because you are not working very hard and your body does not need to produce much energy. Then as your power output increases so too does your VO_2. However, notice that at the end of the test your VO_2 stops rising even though your power output continues to increase. This plateau in VO_2 is the classic sign that you have reached your VO_2max. In addition to measuring your VO_2max this test also determines the power output you reach at the end. This maximum aerobic power output is the highest power output that you produced during the test. It is measured only for the last minute of the test so it is sometimes referred to as 'maximum minute power output'. This power output is significant as it denotes the highest power output you can produce aerobically. For endurance events, your maximum minute power output represents the highest power output that you can reasonably be expected to sustain for any length of time. You would not expect to exceed your maximum aerobic power output except for short efforts. When you use your power meter in training or during an event, you can judge how hard you have ridden by how close to your maximum aerobic power output you were.

By knowing your VO_2max and maximum aerobic power output, in other words your engine size, you can also gauge your fitness.

GET LAB TESTED

With a power meter fitted, your bicycle becomes a mobile exercise testing laboratory. However, there are times when it is still useful to perform a standardized laboratory test. Laboratory testing offers the chance to collect measurements that are not easy out on the road, such as your expired gases and your blood lactate profile. It is also a more standardized and reproducible environment for situations where you want to measure relatively modest changes in your fitness or physiological responses.

Ultimately your performance is determined by the power output you can produce during your event. Your power meter gives you an excellent measure of this where it matters: on the road. But laboratory testing allows you to break down and analyse how you produce this power output in terms of your VO_2max, your efficiency and your wider metabolic response to exercise.

If you are interested in a laboratory test it is worth contacting your local university to see if they offer such a service. Many universities with a sports science laboratory will be happy to arrange an exercise test or scientific consultation for you and they can be surprisingly good value.

Table 3. PREDICTED VO$_2$ MAX

Maximum Minute Power (W)	Predicted VO$_2$ max	Predicted ml/kg for 50 kg	Predicted ml/kg for 60 kg	Predicted ml/kg for 70 kg	Predicted ml/kg for 80 kg	Predicted ml/kg for 90 kg	Predicted ml/kg for 100 kg
180	2.20	44.1	36.7	31.5	27.6	24.5	22.0
200	2.44	48.8	40.7	34.9	30.5	27.1	24.4
220	2.68	53.5	44.6	38.2	33.5	29.7	26.8
240	2.91	58.2	48.5	41.6	36.4	32.4	29.1
260	3.15	63.0	52.5	45.0	39.4	35.0	31.5
280	3.38	67.7	56.4	48.3	42.3	37.6	33.8
300	3.62	72.4	60.3	51.7	45.3	40.2	36.2
320	3.86	77.1	64.3	55.1	48.2	42.8	38.6
340	4.09	81.8	68.2	58.5	51.2	45.5	40.9
360	4.33	86.6	72.1	61.8	54.1	48.1	43.3
380	4.56	91.3	76.1	65.2	57.1	50.7	45.6
400	4.80	96.0	80.0	68.6	60.0	53.3	48.0
420	5.04	100.7	83.9	71.9	63.0	56.0	50.4
440	5.27	105.4	87.9	75.3	65.9	58.6	52.7
460	5.51	110.2	91.8	78.7	68.9	61.2	55.1
480	5.74	114.9	95.7	82.1	71.8	63.8	57.4
500	5.98	119.6	99.7	85.4	74.8	66.4	59.8

The more oxygen you can consume the more power you can produce, and the more power you can produce the faster you can ride. Given these relationships you will not be surprised to find that the best riders in the world tend to have the highest VO$_2$max and the greatest maximum aerobic power output.

While laboratory testing is excellent if you want to get your aerobic fitness assessed accurately, fitting your bike with a power meter enables you to get a handle on most of the key elements of your fitness without the time and expense of a laboratory visit. Table 3 shows the results of some of my early research to provide the information you need to calculate your VO$_2$max using just your power meter. You can use this test to monitor changes in your fitness and verify your training is working. From the test you will be able to measure your maximum minute power output and VO$_2$max. Because these tests are widely conducted, you can compare your values with other riders and get a benchmark of your overall level of fitness. You should also reach your maximum heart rate in the test. Knowing your maximum heart rate is useful for setting and monitoring your training heart rate data.

CALCULATING VO$_2$MAX

Measuring your aerobic fitness means maximal exercise on your part, so please do not attempt it if you have any reason for thinking it may not be safe for you to do so. It is best to complete the test on a turbo trainer or ergometer rather than out on the road. Your aim is to replicate the pattern of the test results shown in Figure 6.

After a warm-up, start the test by riding on your turbo trainer and increasing your power output at the end of each minute. You can change gears or increase your resistance to help you work harder. Try to stick closely to the target power output (to within just a few watts). Keep riding harder and harder each minute until you are unable to produce the target power output. By the end of your test you should have reached your maximum heart rate and produced your maximum aerobic power output. You may find it helpful to test yourself with someone else present to guide and encourage you. Women should start at around 120W and increase by 15W every minute. Men usually start a little higher and increase by 20W every minute. Your test should last about 10 minutes; if it is considerably longer or shorter than this then adjust your starting power output accordingly. Do not change the 15W or 20W per minute increase for women and men respectively.

Once you have finished your test, download your power meter and look for the highest power output that you averaged for a full 60 seconds during the test (maximum minute power output). Check that this is a realistic power output for your test by comparing your actual test duration with what you would expect from following the protocol. As an example, imagine your test started at 160W and lasted exactly 10 minutes, increasing at 20W per minute. Your maximum minute power output should be the average from minutes nine to ten (in order words 350W). Look too for your maximum heart rate in the last minute of the test. Ask yourself if it looks plausible compared with values that you have seen recently in training. If it is a bit lower than you expected this might indicate that you did not quite give 100 per cent in the test. You could decide to retest a few days later to see if you can reach an even higher power output.

Once you are satisfied that your maximum minute power output is realistic, use my calculations in Table 3 to estimate your VO$_2$max. The predicted ml/kg figures in Table 3 give the VO$_2$max values for different body weights.

Please note you do not need to conduct these tests in order to determine your TIBs or train effectively with your power meter. As you can train with your power meter every day, you no longer need to include periodic laboratory testing as part of establishing and monitoring your training. But as many riders are interested to find out their VO$_2$max and gauge their aerobic fitness using their power meter, the details are described in the box.

It is not possible to measure your endurance in the way that you can use VO$_2$max to quantify your aerobic fitness. There is not a specific test for endurance fitness so it is not possible to go to a sports science laboratory and get your endurance fitness measured (although, as I mentioned previously, some people do not distinguish between aerobic and endurance fitness and regard VO_2max as a measure of endurance).

In laboratory experiments I sometimes use a time-to-exhaustion test as an indicator of endurance performance. To complete the test you have to ride for as long as possible at a fixed power output. The test ends when you become exhausted and unable to continue. Your endurance performance is recorded as the time you lasted before exhaustion. Whilst this is a useful protocol for experiments it does not provide a helpful measure of endurance fitness. The reason for this is because your time to exhaustion is mostly determined by your power output or relative intensity. If your power output is low you will of course be able to ride for a long time, whereas at a high work rate your time to exhaustion is short. Therefore you cannot establish a simple single measure

of endurance fitness as it varies across different training intensities.

When you ride in different TIBs you are also varying the length of time you can train. Let us look at what happens in terms of your endurance (how long you can ride). Figure 7 shows the relationship between your training intensity and duration. The horizontal axis shows the length of your ride (in other words its time or distance) and the vertical axis is your power output. To interpret it, imagine you have been asked to produce the highest power output you possibly can for just a few seconds. This provides the left-most point on the graph. Now imagine you have been asked to do the same thing but over the whole of a ride lasting several hours. This provides the right-most point on the graph.

The shape of the curve between these two extremes shows what would happen

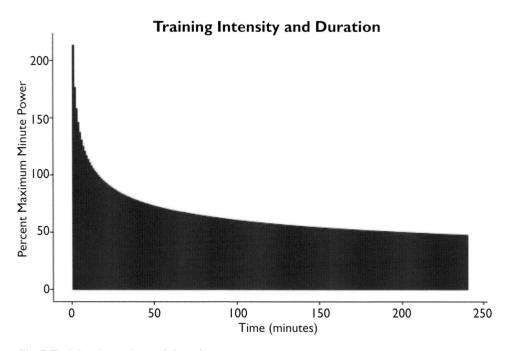

Fig. 7 Training intensity and duration.

if you were asked to ride for the specific length of time in between. Notice that you can produce very high power outputs for very short rides. As the length of the ride increases the power output you can sustain falls away rapidly. Then you reach a point where your power output hardly changes despite a substantial increase in the length of your ride. This curve shows the relationship between exercise intensity (the TIBs) and the length of your training session. From this Figure you can probably work out why there is not a standard test for endurance fitness: how long you can ride will depend primarily upon your target power output, not your endurance fitness *per se*.

Take a moment to familiarize yourself with the nature of the relationship between your work rate and the time you can sustain in training. It's called an exponential curve. Focus especially on power outputs below your maximum minute power output because the majority of your power meter data will be gathered from training at these intensities. Whenever you look at your training in detail you will see that it is constrained by the shape of this curve. As you train with your power meter you will learn from experience where the line is for you. For example, you will come to know the power output you can manage for a five-minute effort. Then you will also be able to anticipate how your power output needs to change when you double the length of your effort to ten minutes. Similarly, you will start to notice how your power output changes as a consequence of your training. As you get fitter the average power output of your rides will begin to creep up. You should also deliberately mix up your training by riding at different points on your curve. Some days get used to riding faster by including

shorter, high-intensity efforts or training sessions. On other days stretch out your ride and lower your intensity to build your endurance instead. Getting a feel for how the intensity of your training changes as you alter the length of your rides will help you plan different training sessions effectively.

Some coaches and scientists describe the exponential relationship in Figure 7 as if there is a 'threshold' for longer rides, as mentioned in Chapter 5. When your power output is below this threshold you can sustain your effort for a long time, but once you have crossed the threshold you will quickly start to fatigue and be forced to ease up or stop. You can see how this happens if you look at Figure 8 (an annotated version of Figure 7) and imagine that you are completing an hour-long ride. To complete this training ride you will probably choose to ride at somewhere near 70 per cent of your maximum on the graph. Now consider what happens if you were to increase your power output by 10 per cent to 80 per cent of your maximum. You are now riding at a power output that you cannot sustain for anywhere near as long. Follow the arrows as they show how this change in your power output reduces how long you can keep going at this increased power output. The reduction in how long you can keep training is quite dramatic from 60 minutes to only 35 minutes. You can probably imagine that it would feel almost as if you have crossed a threshold, and that at 80 per cent you are riding at an intensity that you are unable to sustain for an extended length of time. This is important to consider when quantifying training overload.

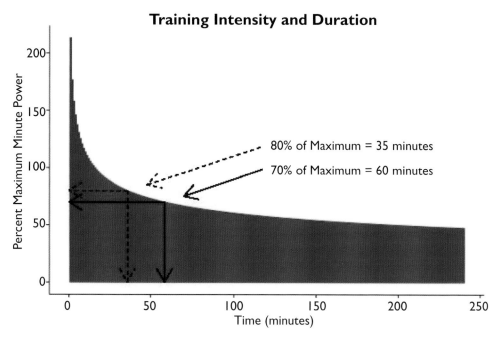

Fig. 8 Training intensity and duration (annotated).

QUANTIFYING TRAINING OVERLOAD

By now the importance of applying an overload in training in order to get fitter should be clear. Equally important is to be able to quantify your training overload. Using TIBs makes quantifying your overload straightforward. Most of the time you will probably only need to think about the training you do in terms of TIBs and this is fine. But it is sometimes helpful to be familiar with how your overload is quantified in order to fine tune this process and get the most from your training. The primary components of your training overload are your training intensity (the specific TIB), training duration and training frequency. An increment in any of these components, either individually or in combination, increases your training

overload. The fact that you can measure and monitor all three of these components of your overload with your power meter is what makes it such a prime training tool.

Your training intensity defines how hard you are working during your training session. When you train with a power meter you can describe your training intensity in terms of the power output for that session. However, riders with different levels of fitness will perceive the same power output very differently. Therefore it is often necessary to consider not only the absolute intensity but the relative training intensity for each individual too. The challenge of riding at 250W is likely to feel different for every rider. This is because it is an absolute intensity and differences in fitness will also alter how easy it is to accomplish. In contrast riding at a relative intensity of 70 per cent of maximum power output should

Italian rider Elia Viviani at the USA Pro Cycling Challenge in Denver, Colorado.

feel very similar for most riders regardless of their fitness. The absolute training intensity takes no account of differences between riders whilst the relative intensity is adjusted to feel the same for every rider.

The differences between absolute and relative intensity can be quite marked because elite riders are capable of generating and maintaining extremely high power outputs. Consequently an elite rider can ride quite comfortably at a power output

that a sub-elite rider cannot achieve at all. For example, I normally find riding at 250W to be close to my maximum race pace for a time trial or long hill climb. The winner of the Tour de France, on the other hand, will ride the whole three-week race at around this power output and on some days will average considerably more. In contrast, the majority of non-cyclists cannot manage to sustain 250W at all. Clearly as 250W will feel very different to these people you would not give everyone this same absolute training intensity or expect similar results if you did.

Using a relative training intensity, however, the situation is different. Training at 75 per cent is likely to feel about the same regardless of whether you are a Tour de France champion or you hardly ride your bike at all. When you set your TIBs you are actually calculating your relative training intensities. This is how the same system of TIBs can work similarly for most riders. Equally, if you find that they do not feel quite as I have described them, do not be afraid to make a small adjustment to them. Although in theory a relative training intensity is the same for different riders, in practice no two people respond to training identically, not even twins.

Your training duration is how long your training session lasts and is measured in terms of distance or time. Your training overload will increase as you make your training sessions longer. Previously I explained that your training intensity is the main factor that dictates how long you can train. At very high (sprint) intensities, trying to add a few seconds to your training duration will be extremely challenging, whilst at a low training intensity you may experience little difficulty in training for an extra twenty or thirty minutes. This is the exponential relationship between your training duration and intensity shown in Figure 7.

When I first started in sports science, on-the-bike heart rate monitors and power meters were not available, therefore riders could not measure their intensity when they were riding their bikes in training. Consequently riders and coaches tended to think about training in terms of volume, in other words in terms of miles. With the advent of heart rate monitors and power meters you can now measure your training intensity and so it makes sense to quantify your training duration in time rather than distance in most situations.

Training frequency refers to how often you train, and is usually expressed in terms of the number of sessions per week. Typically most riders who want to improve their fitness or performance will train at least twice a week, but the type of training you complete influences the frequency you can manage as more demanding sessions require longer recovery. Nonetheless, space your training sessions too far apart and the reversibility principle will mean that you have lost the benefits of each session before you start the next. Conversely, if you increase your training frequency you will magnify your training overload and reduce your recovery time. This is therefore a potent way of boosting your training overload. So be careful if you increase your training frequency: you will need to monitor your feelings of tiredness and fatigue carefully and rest if they increase notably.

Sometimes you may also hear riders or coaches discussing training overload in terms of training volume and training load. Training volume is an indication of how much training you are doing. Your training volume is the combination of your training duration and training frequency (how long and how often you train). You increase your training volume by riding longer or training more often. Training volume does not take account of the TIB you are riding in your training and it is therefore of limited value. Consequently, it is generally more useful to think about your training load. Training load is the combination of all three overload training components: intensity, duration and frequency (or you can think of it as training volume and intensity). Including intensity makes a big difference to your training overload. For example, you will notice the effects of adding short high-intensity sessions to your programme even if you already have quite a high training volume.

When you train with your power meter and use TIBs you can keep track of your overload simply. All you need to know in order to monitor your overload is the time spent in each TIB. There are several websites and GPS and power meter programs that can help do this for you, and many of them are free to use. One of the benefits of using TIBs is that monitoring your training overload becomes straightforward, and therefore you do not need to think about technical definitions of training volume and load or how to calculate them for your power meter data.

CHAPTER SEVEN

ESTABLISHING YOUR TRAINING INTENSITY BANDS

Establishing your TIBs is very straightforward, although it takes some physical effort on your part. You complete a twenty-minute standardized ride with your power meter. Using the average power output from this ride you then calculate all your TIBs from Table 4. It is simple! I will go through this protocol in a little more detail but first I will explain how it can be so simple.

GETTING TIBs RIGHT

Your TIBs are a convenient way for us to describe the intensity of your training, not how your body works. The boundaries between one TIB and the next have little physiological importance. As you cross a boundary between one TIB and the next your body cannot 'notice'. In reality your training intensity works on a more complicated continuum from low to maximum training intensities, and from short to long training sessions (*refer back to* Figure 7). The TIBs are a practical means of chopping this continuum into useful training-session sized chunks. Similarly, your body will not adapt markedly differently in response to small differences in your training intensity. The

training process is simply not that precise (or at least our current scientific understanding of it is not). Your response to training is governed by a complex interaction of physical, mental, social, environmental and other factors. How these factors interact is and will probably remain too complex for us to appreciate fully. Using TIBs helps to reduce this complexity into a useful training strategy.

Do take care in how you calculate your TIBs but be mindful that it is not an exact science. Keep in mind too that your fitness will inevitably vary day to day, and more importantly that your aim is to change your TIBs substantially over a period of time with training. This means that your TIBs are sufficiently flexible to cope with noticeable changes in your fitness and remain usable. Overall you are aiming to establish and work with TIBs as a helpful, descriptive framework for your training with your power meter. They provide simple and convenient labels to help you describe, record and analyse your training. Nonetheless, if after reading this book you feel you need more detailed or personalized guidance on setting your TIBs and training effectively, it may be worth seeking the help of a coach or going to a sports science laboratory for testing.

Table 4. TRAINING INTENSITY BAND.

	% 20 min power	From	Target	To
TIB1 – Recovery	Up to 56%	0 W	N/A	148 W
TIB2 – Moderate	56 to 70%	148 W	167 W	186 W
TIB3 – Tempo	70 to 90%	176 W	202 W	238 W
TIB4 – Race pace	90 to 120%	238 W	278 W	317 W
TIB5 – Intervals	120 to 160%	317 W	371 W	424 W
TIB6 – Top end	160 to 215%	424 W	497 W	569 W
TIB7 – Sprint	215 > 280%	569 W	664 W	759 W

Example based on a rider with 20 minute power of 265 W

STRAIGHTENING THE CURVE

Previously I introduced the exponential curve that describes the relationship between your training intensity and training duration, shown in Figure 7. I observed that you can maintain a high power output typical of TIB6 and TIB7 for only a short period of time. As your training time increases the power output you can sustain decreases rapidly and disproportionately. Once your training is reduced to the moderate intensities of TIB2 and TIB3 this relationship flattens out. At this level relatively large increases in your training time can be achieved with only small reductions in your power output. This exponential relationship between training time and intensity is found for everyone. Indeed it is also apparent for most other types of training you might perform, for example for rowing, running and swimming, and even in different animals such as horses.

This predictable relationship is particularly helpful when it comes to setting TIBs. From my previous research and findings with other riders' training I do not even need lots of data to predict your curve. Because this predictable relationship exists I already know the shape of your curve without having to measure all of it. This means you do not need to perform extensive tests in a sports science laboratory to identify your training time–intensity curve. Instead, just one or two reference points on your curve are sufficient; once I have them on your curve I can easily calculate your TIBs.

CALCULATING YOUR TIBs

As I said at the beginning of this chapter, calculating your TIBs is straightforward. You ride very hard for twenty minutes with your power meter, then use the average power output from this ride to calculate your TIBs using Table 4. The average power output from this ride provides the necessary reference point allowing your training time–intensity curve to be defined. Table 4 then helps you chop this curve into your separate TIBs.

Your standardized twenty-minute ride is obviously critical for determining your TIBs, therefore you should take reasonable care in how you perform this. However, because the process is so simple and the ride is used to calculate your TIBs, not to measure your fitness, you do not need to be too concerned about getting it wrong. After all it is easy to repeat the whole procedure on a regular basis should you wish to. You need to be reasonably fresh and ready to perform, but not necessarily at 100 per cent. Similarly, although you are measuring the highest average power output you can sustain in your standardized test ride, you do not need to try and squeeze out every last watt. You are looking to produce a good, solid ride that provides a clear indication of what you are capable of over twenty minutes. You should treat the test ride as a demanding training session; you need not prepare for it and ride it as if it is a race. For this reason it is fine to perform the twenty-minute test within a longer training session; just make sure that you do it near the beginning.

Perform the test ride on a quiet road where you can make a sustained twenty-minute effort safely and without interruption from other road users. If you do not have an appropriate road nearby you can use an indoor static trainer. The ideal road is reasonably flat or only gently undulating, on which you can maintain a constant power output throughout. If you use a stationary trainer use the same power meter that you will be using in your subsequent training to ensure consistency. Before the test ride take the time to warm-up thoroughly, and also to perform a couple of sprints at 90 per cent effort. Start your power meter recording at the beginning of the ride and stop it after exactly twenty minutes.

At the beginning of the ride start in a very controlled manner and aim to keep an even pace, building your power output over the second 10 minutes if possible. After your ride, download your power meter and note your average power output. This power output should be the highest or within a few watts of the highest that you are able to sustain for twenty minutes. If you think you can do substantially better, just repeat the test again on a different day.

Once you have established the highest average power output you can sustain for twenty minutes you can use this information to calculate your TIBs. I have already done most of the work in the calculations underpinning Table 4. Each TIB is calculated as a percentage of your twenty-minute average power output. Table 4 also provides an example calculation. For this example I have assumed your maximum twenty-minute average power output is 265W. All you need to do is substitute your actual twenty-minute average power output values into this example.

Substituting your TIBs into Table 4 is also straightforward. Use your twenty-minute test average power output to calculate the top of TIB1 by multiplying it by 0.56 (in other words by 56 per cent). In the case of the example in Table 4 the calculation is 265W × 0.56 = 148W. This power output denotes the top of one TIB and it also forms the bottom of the next TIB. Therefore 148W is not only the top of TIB1 but also the bottom of TIB2.

The top of TIB2 is calculated by multiplying by 0.7 your twenty-minute test average power output. Hence in Table 4 the calculation is 265W × 0.7 = 186W. As before, this value forms the top of TIB2 and the bottom of TIB3. Continue to calculate the power output for the top of each of the remaining TIBs in the same way (0.9 for TIB3, 1.2 for TIB4, 1.6 for TIB5 and 2.15 for TIB6). The final thing you should do is to write down each of your TIBs and calculate their midpoint. This is labelled as the 'Target' in Table 4. You have now established your personalized TIBs and are ready to start using them in training.

If you want to check that your TIBs have been calculated correctly, you can do so by performing a further test or 'calibration' ride. Two measurements are normally more accurate than one, so if you are unsure as to whether you have established your TIBs correctly it is worth double check-ing. As with calculating your original TIBs, it is simple but even quicker to do. The principle is exactly the same as before, but instead you measure your five-minute average power output. Your average power output for five minutes should be notably higher than your twenty-minute power output. Use your twenty-minute average power output value to check against your previously calculated TIB5 values. Your five-minute average power output should fall just inside TIB5, in other words above the bottom but below the target power output for the mid-range of this TIB. In the example provided in Table 4, the five-minute power output is expected to be around 320W. You will see that this places it just inside TIB5, above the bottom (317W) but considerably less than the mid-range (371W) target. If this is the case you need not do anything further: your calibration check has passed.

If you calculate that you are more than 15W out, first perform your twenty-min-ute test again to make sure that you have an accurate value from which to calculate your TIBs. If after retesting your twenty-min-ute average power output the discrepancy between your five-minute average power output and your calculated TIB5 remains, it is best to adjust your TIBs manually. To make the adjustment, use your five-minute average power output to replace the predicted value for the bottom of your TIB5. As you replace the bottom of TIB5 note how much it has changed from the value calculated from your twenty-minute average power output. Now change the bottom of TIB6 and TIB7 by the same amount. You do not need to adjust TIB1 to TIB4 as your twenty-minute average power output provides a better basis for calculating these. There are several reasons why a manual adjustment may be needed. The main one is that no two riders are iden-tical and you may need your TIBs set slightly differently to reflect this.

Many websites and most power meter software will calculate your maximum five-minute and twenty-minute performance from each ride for you, even when you have not performed these specific tests. Although this is not quite as good as per-forming the specific test, it provides a useful interim value until you get the chance to test yourself properly. If you spot that you have achieved a higher value than was used to set your TIBs, you can change your TIBs to reflect this. Alternatively you can use it as a reminder that it could be time to reset your TIBs by retesting (see the next section).

I have also created a website that will help you calculate your TIBs and provides other resources and information related to train-ing with your power meter. This is available at www.trainingwithpowermeters.co.uk

REPEAT TESTING

I mentioned previously that your TIBs are personal to you and depend on your level of fitness. This also means that as your fitness changes so should your TIBs. Your TIBs are quite broad so you should not need to keep updating them all the time, but you will need to adjust them periodically or whenever your fitness changes markedly.

You will recognize when your TIBs need adjusting by referring to the middle value of each band. The middle of each TIB provides a target power output. Ideally, your TIB and this middle value should be challenging and realistic. This means that the middle of each TIB occurs at a power output that is little higher than you can comfortably manage. As you get fitter your average power output for each training session should progress toward and then beyond the middle of its TIB. Eventually you may find that you are able to train consistently above the midpoint in your TIB. Once this happens it is the signal that it is time to consider readjusting your TIBs. Do this by repeating your standardized twenty-minute test and recalculating your TIBs.

After you have readjusted your TIBs you should once again find that the midpoint of the TIB provides a challenging target for your training sessions. It should constitute a target that you will have to work towards over a period of time.

Do not forget that your TIBs may need to come down as well as be pushed up. When you suspect that your fitness has dropped you may need to retest in order to lower your TIBs. This may occur if you have had a period of easier or lighter training, or perhaps if you have not been able to train for a while. Once you resume training you may find you need to build back up gradually. If you find that you are struggling to maintain the power output associated with your specified TIBs or are fatiguing faster than normal, it's probably time to readjust your TIBs.

Whichever way you think you may need to adjust your TIBs, including a hard five- or twenty-minute effort in your next training session, it will give you a further feel for whether your TIBs need to be properly retested.

CHAPTER EIGHT

TRAINING WITH YOUR POWER METER

RIDING WITH YOUR POWER METER

Watching your power meter as you ride, you will notice that your power output fluctuates rapidly. At times it can almost seem as if you are not in control of your power output at all. Try not to be distracted by these inevitable variations in your power output as you ride. Instead focus on accumulating riding time in your target TIB. Over time you should find that you become more effective in reducing these fluctuations in your power output. Nonetheless, rather than strive to hold a specific power output (for example 250W), focus on training within your relevant TIB (for example between 230W and 270W). It is your average power output and where this sits within your specified TIB that you should focus on. Figure 9 shows the power output for an elite rider completing a four-hour training ride. During this session the rider was generally working in TIB2 and added two efforts at TIB4 on long climbs. Even with all the variability in power output during the ride you can spot the two TIB4 efforts quite clearly by the way the rider's average power output has risen for that effort.

Once you finish your ride you can download your power meter and look at the time spent in your target TIB. Your initial aim is to ensure that a significant proportion of your ride is spent within your target TIB. With practice, you can ride more smoothly and flatten out some of the fluctuations in power output. By reading the road ahead you can gauge your effort accordingly. On descents you will find that your power output tends to drop away as your speed rises. Without taking unnecessary risks try to chase this power up when possible. Riding fast and powerfully downhill is a skill. It needs to be practised and developed, and can feel quite odd at first.

Conversely, climbing up a hill you will find your power output tends to increase inadvertently. Here it is important for you to learn how to measure your effort evenly and hold back near the bottom. When you are on controlled rides try to change your speed with the gradient in order to keep your power output constant, rather than trying to keep your speed constant. As the gradient levels off, you can change up a gear and accelerate away rather than labouring over the top as you get your breath back. Over time you will notice that this way of riding feels less stressful and faster. Of course, very steep hills mean

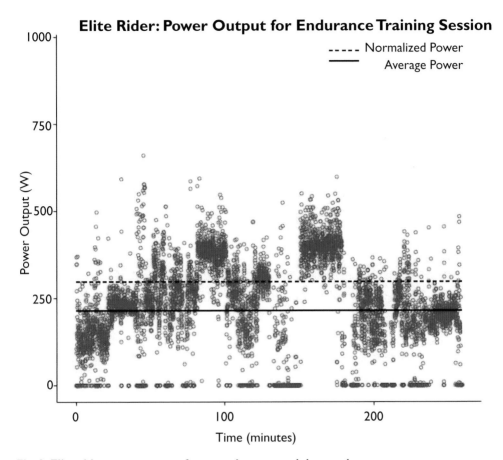

Fig. 9 Elite rider power output for an endurance training session.

it is impossible to hold a constant power without going too slowly.

Riding on windy days presents a similar challenge. Riding fast with a tail wind you will notice makes it difficult to keep to your desired training overload. Here having a power meter pays off as you can quickly see whether you are maintaining your target TIB work rate. Training in this way, you will find that you start to develop a feel for riding at constant work rates. Then as riding conditions change you can alter your effort in order to hold a consistent power output without always having to

think or check your power meter directly. Riding smoothly like this helps you make the most of your training. If your main event is a sportive or a time-trial it is good practice for these too. However, if you regularly race against other riders and in a bunch then you will need to regularly ride in a different way too. In road racing and mountain biking, you have to make efforts that disrupt your rivals, or that follow their moves when they try to do this to you. In these situations you will not be able to ride smoothly and so should practise this in training too.

Feedback from your power meter will help you make sure that your training overload is maintained in every session.

TRAINING FOR AEROBIC AND ENDURANCE FITNESS

The foundation for most types of cycling event is to have good aerobic and endurance fitness. This general rule applies if the event you are preparing for is more than about two-minutes long. The events which tend not to require a high emphasis on endurance or aerobic fitness are BMX, MTB downhill, and sprint-based track races. For most other events your aerobic and endurance fitness is key.

Both endurance and aerobic fitness can be developed on a programme of predominately TIB2 and TIB3 training sessions. Therefore, before considering the preparation for specific events or disciplines in Chapter 9, I will discuss training for aerobic and endurance fitness more generically. The universal aspects of developing aerobic and endurance fitness apply regardless of whether ultimately you are preparing to train for a sportive, a road race, a triathlon or a time trial.

If you have not done much cycling recently you will find that your fitness can improve noticeably by training for one to two hours at TIB2. Training just twice a week can be sufficient for you to feel and notice rapid and sizable improvements in your riding. As you progress, your training sessions will need to do the same. I have outlined previously that your training overload has three components: the duration, intensity and frequency of your training. Therefore your training overload can be increased in these three different ways:

- increase the length of your training sessions
- increase the intensity of your training sessions
- increase the number of training sessions you complete in a week.

Let us consider each of these options in turn.

Increasing the length of your training sessions

Increasing the length of your training sessions by riding further is a relatively straightforward way of ensuring progression in your training. It is both easy and satisfying to track your progress as you watch your mileage stack up in your power meter records.

One of the key aspects of training effectively is how much training time you accumulate at the target training intensities. Elite riders in a heavy endurance-training block can complete long rides of five to seven hours, day after day, at the peak of their training. Critical to this approach though is the intensity of the training you are accumulating. For your long rides to be a worthwhile use of your time you should still be training at TIB2 or above. Always keep in mind that you perform well by riding faster, not further. Do not sacrifice the average power output of your training rides simply for the sake of training longer.

Increasing the intensity of your training sessions

Another way of adding progression to your training overload is by increasing your power output. When training in TIB2 and TIB3 it is generally better to train at a higher power output rather than at a lower power output for longer. Your increased power output will result in you riding faster as your training sessions progress. Over the course of your training blocks, look to increment your average power output for similar sessions. This progression will help you make sure that your training overload is maintained in every session.

A particularly effective way of pursuing these incremental gains is to use the feedback from your power meter as you train. Before the start of your training session, calculate the average power output from your previous similar session. Then use the average from the previous as a target for the current one. Your aim is to nudge the average of your current session slightly above that of the previous one. You can coax incremental improvements from your body much like you encouraging a donkey by dangling a carrot on a stick. As you nudge up your training, watch that you keep your rides within the appropriate TIB. Incrementing your average power output within the specific TIB in this way is an effective way of pushing up your fitness, but resist the temptation to allow your endurance rides to become time trials. This can happen easily if you allow your power meter numbers alone to determine your training targets.

If you aggressively push up your average training power output, you can inadvertently allow your rides to move from TIB2 into TIB3. Do not confuse training in a different TIB from the one you planned with readjusting your TIBs because you are fitter – this is not the same. For this reason it is best to plan training increments within short individual training blocks (see Chapter 11). Also employ increments for only one type of training session (not for every one). Start the block in a very controlled manner and gently increment the intensity to build your training overload progressively.

Increasing the number of training sessions you complete in a week

You can systematically progress in your aerobic and endurance training overload by incrementing the length of your training sessions and the average power output for your training sessions, as we have seen. Nonetheless, your progression within both training duration and intensity has to halt. What then? It is then time to manipulate your training frequency, the third component in your training overload.

When you first started training you may have found that your recovery took longer compared with more experienced riders, especially after a long or challenging training session. You might have found that after a weekend that included two rides your legs were still feeling the after effects in mid-week. In contrast some of the others you were riding with are happily putting in another long training ride, seemingly impervious to the fatiguing effects of a hard weekend of training.

Over a period of time, though, you should find that your recovery starts to accelerate. This occurs because your training rides begin to feel easier and as you get fitter each ride takes less out of you. One of the important responses to endurance training is that your body will upgrade its ability to resist training fatigue and to recover faster from it. As you accumulate the benefit of these adaptations you can start to increase the frequency with which you train.

When you first begin increasing the number of training sessions you perform in a week, compensate for the increased number by reducing the amount of training you do in each session. Only reintroduce longer or more intense training rides once you have adjusted to training with a greater frequency.

It is also critical when you train more frequently that you not only think about the current training session but about how you will manage the next few too. With an increased number of training sessions you must manage how hard you train over a whole block, not simply from session to session. In particular, be aware of the repercussions of your recovery after a hard training session on the remainder of your training plan. Sometimes you will have to deliberately hold back in your training,

not to ensure that you can complete the current session but to allow yourself to recover sufficiently for the next one. This is the way that the top riders can manage impressive volumes of training. For the top riders in full training, twenty to thirty hours a week would not be considered exceptional. But training for this length of time five, six or sometimes even seven days a week can only work successfully if they manage their recovery carefully from one day to the next. Even for them, if they overstep the mark in training on one day then they will not just spoil the objectives for that training session but also those for the following day and beyond.

Assessing your aerobic and endurance training needs

Without sufficient aerobic fitness, you will not be able to ride fast enough to stay with your training group or the race peloton. If your endurance is lacking you will find that you regularly run out of steam before the end of the race. But when you are struggling in races it can be hard to decide whether you need to train for more aerobic fitness by riding faster, or for more endurance by riding longer.

Your power meter is very helpful in this regard. Use it to monitor your power output in long rides or races. Then you can replay the ride and examine what power output you were trying to sustain. If the power output you were trying to hold was greater than your training power output in TIB3 and TIB4 then your aerobic fitness is the thing to focus on in training. This is the most common situation for road racers. However, if you find that the power output you require has not changed notably but still you have started to struggle, this is a sign that your endurance is lacking.

If you are unsure whether to focus on aerobic or endurance fitness always go for the former, adopting a 'train to ride fast rather than further' approach. There are two reasons for this recommendation. Firstly, riders who increase their aerobic fitness normally find they have better endurance as a consequence, but the converse does not always apply. As an example, consider you are struggling to stay with your training group on a long ride because you are working constantly at 70 per cent or more of your maximum minute power output. Increasing your aerobic fitness by 10 per cent will mean the same ride becomes much easier as it represents only 60 per cent of your maximum. Now you find the effort a lot less demanding and staying with your training group becomes less daunting. But you have achieved this by changing your aerobic fitness rather than your endurance.

The second reason is that endurance tends to be much easier to gain than aerobic fitness, therefore you are less likely to lack endurance. And if you do lack endurance you can usually rectify this quite quickly by increasing the length of your training rides.

STRUCTURING INTERVAL SESSIONS FOR TIB5, TIB6 AND TIB7

Power meters are a super tool for monitoring your training in TIB5, TIB6 and TIB7. At these TIBs only a power meter gives you an accurate reflection of how hard you are working. Typically, these training sessions will consist of high-intensity periods

of riding punctuated with easier recovery periods. Coaches and scientists normally refer to this as interval training.

With interval training you plan not only the work periods but also the recovery periods. The factors to consider when structuring your TIB5, TIB6 or TIB7 session intervals are their total number, the length and intensity of the work periods, and the length and intensity of the recovery periods. Design your intervals to enable you to accumulate more time at your target training intensity compared with performing continuous training. Simultaneously, try to provide a training overload to your physiological systems that is not possible at lower TIBs. The intensity of each of your intervals is dictated by its TIB, but the duration of each interval and your target number of intervals can be infinitely varied. Experiment with different permutations in an attempt to maximize your training effect.

The intervals and recovery parameters need to be considered together with the overall aim of the session. There are two broad strategies that you can choose between for interval training. The first of these two strategies is to build your ability to reproduce high-intensity efforts. Here your aim is to accumulate high-intensity training time by performing a number of shorter efforts. As each interval is quite short, your recovery does not need to be very long to allow you to successfully complete another interval. Therefore the structure that evolves for these types of session is short intervals and a short recovery period. These intervals can often be repeated many times.

The second type of interval session structure is designed to induce maximum power and fatigue. In the previous interval structure, the point at which you fail or struggle to produce the required power output is the point at which you should stop. Here, in contrast, your aim is to learn to cope with this sensation of a maximum effort and your legs progressively tying up. To do this you will need to specify longer intervals, as short intervals would be over before you really experience fatigue. Training in the face of increasing fatigue like this is mentally and physically very demanding, so you need a reasonable recovery between efforts. This enables some of the fatigue from the previous effort to dissipate. It also allows you time to refocus and commit to the next effort. Efforts like this can only be repeated a limited number of times before you will experience a very marked drop in quality of effort or your commitment to them. Therefore you might aim to perform between two and four repetitions. Ideally, you should try to focus entirely on the interval you are performing. By restricting the number of repetitions you perform, you do not need to be distracted by thinking about how many intervals are remaining or what the next effort will feel like. Towards the end of each of these intervals you will expect to struggle to maintain the required power output, but in this instance that is a desired effect. However, if you cannot reach your target power, or your average for the interval drops below your TIB range, then you should stop.

Heart rate and high-intensity intervals

Be wary of using heart rate monitors when training in TIB5, TIB6 or TIB7. If you use a heart rate monitor you have probably already noticed that it takes a little while for your heart rate to react to a change in effort. During the prolonged training typical of TIB1 to TIB4 this is not an issue. Indeed, this delay in your heart rate response can act to usefully smooth out the inevitable changes in pace that occur during training: because it smooths out your response you can use your heart rate as an effective guide to your appropriate training intensity. However, for TIB5, TIB6 and TIB7 this delay and smoothing become a hindrance rather than a help. Your heart rate typically takes between thirty seconds and a minute before it begins to reflect your work rate. For most forms of highly structured interval training this means your heart rate cannot be used to provide a useful guide. In contrast, the power output data provided by your power meter provides you with exactly what you need. Indeed your power meter is the only tool useful for monitoring and analysing training that involves TIB5, TIB6 or TIB7.

NORMALIZED POWER OUTPUT

Some power meters and most websites and software will calculate your normalized power output in addition to your average power output. As it is not always immediately obvious what this means, I'll explain.

Normalized power output is a concept to smooth out the variations in your power meter data. The simplest way of smoothing all the variations in your power meter data is to look at your average power output. However, because the variation in power output during your ride can be quite extreme, lots of different ways of indicating this variation have been suggested. Normalized power is one of the most popular ways of indicating the variation in power output during your ride.

To give you an insight into how normalized power output works look at Figure 10. This figure shows two training rides, both with an average power output of 150W. Note how one of these rides was ridden at a consistent power output of 150W, while the other ride comprised intervals at 300W with recovery at 0W. You can probably appreciate that these rides would feel quite different. However, the average power for both rides is the same at 150W. In contrast, if you calculate normalized power output for these two rides you will find they differ markedly. The normalized power for the consistent ride is the same as its average power output. But the normalized power output for the interval session is much higher than its average power output. This is because normalized power output has been designed to reflect the extra physiological

Post-competition discussion. (Snig/Shutterstock.com)

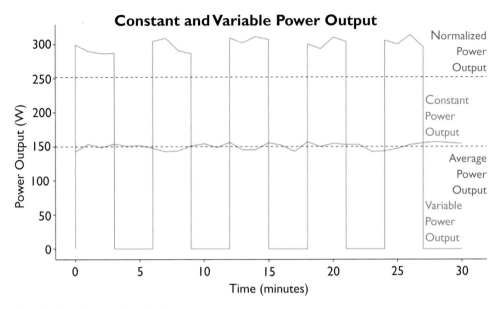

Fig. 10 Constant and variable power output.

stress you experience when your power output varies markedly. If your power output remains very consistent during a ride, then your normalized power will be the same as your average power output.

Therefore, if your normalized power differs markedly from your average power, this is an indication that your power output has been highly variable.

CHAPTER NINE

TRAINING WITH POWER METERS TO IMPROVE PERFORMANCE

The following sections look at some of the specific demands of preparing for different events. The aim of each section is to give some thoughts on the specific challenges of each event and how you can address these when training with your power meter. Appendix 2 also provides some example training blocks for each of the different events. The idea is that you use these for training ideas and tailor them to your specific goals and fitness. Several of the training blocks are designed to develop aerobic and endurance fitness generally. Therefore, although they may be categorized in this book under a specific discipline, you will probably find that they are appropriate for most of the events discussed below.

ROAD RACING

Road races normally tend to be organized over distances of more than 30 miles (and elite ones around 100 miles); this clearly makes them an endurance event. Consequently, the traditional training for many road riders focuses on developing aerobic and endurance fitness as their primary concern. Despite the long race distances, do not become overly preoccupied with developing endurance. Training for successful road racing requires a slightly different mindset than for other cycling events. The reason is that for most other events training to win races is simple (in concept): you need to train to be fitter than your rivals. Whilst in theory being fitter means you will perform better in many cycling events, this does not apply so well in road racing. To win a road race you do not have to be the fittest rider, or even produce a high average power output. Instead you have to use your fitness to go faster than your rivals *at a critical point in the race*. This critical point may be to create or follow a race winning move, perhaps on a climb, into a strong wind or simply when your rivals are not paying attention. If the race finishes as one big bunch then it is the final sprint that decides the outcome. Using your fitness tactically and judging your move well is very important. If you get this right you can regularly outperform people who you know to be fitter than you in general.

At the speeds typical of most road races, up to 90 per cent of your power output goes into overcoming wind resistance. The effect of riding in the bunch or in the slipstream of other riders reduces the wind

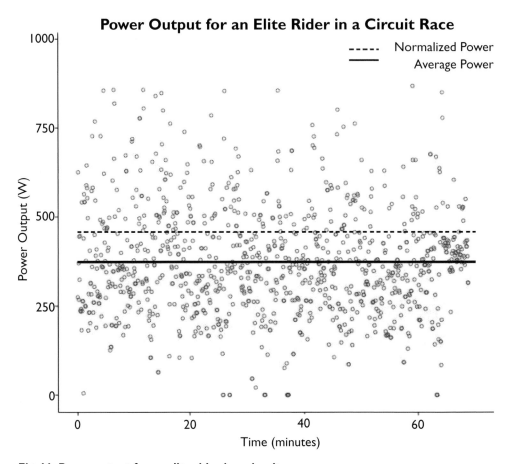

Fig. 11 Power output for an elite rider in a circuit race.

resistance and hence your power output by around 30 per cent. If you can hide in your rivals' slipstream for all but the last few metres of the race then you only need 70 per cent of their aerobic fitness to still have a chance of winning in the final sprint.

The two situations where this does not hold true are when climbing and when accelerating. In both of these situations your power output is being primarily directed to overcoming forces related to your body weight rather than wind resistance. These retarding forces are gravity (when climbing) and inertia (when accelerating). There-

fore if you suspect that your rivals lack your overall aerobic fitness, you can try and expose this by racing up climbs or by making hard accelerations. Equally, you need to be fit enough to cover moves made by your rivals in these situations.

Figure 11 shows the power output for an elite rider in a short circuit road race. You can see that the average power output is high, at well over 300W, and that the power output during the race varies considerably. Consequently, for road racing you need a reasonable VO_2max and sufficient endurance to make it to the end of the race.

Given the importance of tactics in road racing, once you are able regularly to finish with your rivals it is worth training to develop particular race-winning strengths. Use the principle of specificity in your training to develop your fitness specialism. Your aim is to use your specialist fitness to outperform rivals in a critical part of the race. There are a number of aspects of road racing in which you could specialize, such as short climbs, long climbs, time trialling, endurance or sprinting. Keep in mind that you are training your specialism to be faster than the other riders in the race. Pick out just one or two of your relative strengths or abilities to work on and really push this to your limits. To identify your strengths, think about how you compare against your training partners, or look for the point in the race where you tend to go better than your race rivals. Are you someone who enjoys darting away on short climbs? Maybe you cope better powering away on the flat than those around you. Or perhaps you find you can always find a fast sprint no matter how tired you are? Once you have chosen an area to specialize in, make this a regular part of your maintenance programme (see Chapter 10). By doing this you maintain or develop this aspect of your fitness regularly into your overall programme and start the process of training to create winning moves during a race.

CLIMBING

Climbing on your bike is essentially a battle between you and gravity. Every hill or mountain you climb becomes a battleground for this fight. Your performance when you battle with gravity is determined by your power output on the climb and the weight you are lifting up the climb. It is common to express these two terms as your power-to-weight ratio. This ratio is given by the power output you can produce on the climb divided by your combined body and bike weight. The higher your power-to-weight ratio, the faster you will go uphill. Your power to output ratio is measured in W/kg. Because you are lifting the weight of you and your bike to the top of the hill, larger riders are more heavily penalized when climbing. (In contrast, when riding on the flat a larger rider can use the extra power output that comes with size to go faster with much less penalty.) So a 60kg rider might produce a respectable 180W on a long climb for a power-to-weight ratio of $60 \div 180 = 3$W/kg. In contrast, a larger 90kg rider would need to maintain a power output of 270W to match the smaller rider's power-to-weight ratio ($270 \div 90 = 3$W/kg). Table 5 provides examples of how power-to-weight ratios vary for different weights and power outputs.

There are two ways you can raise your power-to-weight ratio and thereby improve your climbing. You can increase the power output you can produce on a climb, or you can reduce the weight of you and your bike. Therefore any training that increases the power output that you can produced when going uphill, or that helps you lose weight, will enable you to climb faster.

On long climbs there is no hiding from the physics of climbing. In these situations your overall aerobic fitness plays the most significant role in dictating how well you can go uphill. As you get fitter you become capable of sustaining a higher power output. This higher power output will allow you to climb faster. Therefore an important aspect of climbing well is to have a high aerobic fitness (VO_2max) and be capable of sustaining a high power output relative to your body weight. Training at

Table 5. POWER WEIGHT CLIMBING

Climbing Power Output (W)	W/kg at 50 kg	W/kg at 60 kg	W/kg at 70 kg	W/kg at 80 kg	W/kg at 90 kg	W/kg at 100 kg
120	2.4	2.0	1.7	1.5	1.3	1.2
140	2.8	2.3	2.0	1.8	1.6	1.4
160	3.2	2.7	2.3	2.0	1.8	1.6
180	3.6	3.0	2.6	2.3	2.0	1.8
200	4.0	3.3	2.9	2.5	2.2	2.0
220	4.4	3.7	3.1	2.8	2.4	2.2
240	4.8	4.0	3.4	3.0	2.7	2.4
260	5.2	4.3	3.7	3.3	2.9	2.6
280	5.6	4.7	4.0	3.5	3.1	2.8
300	6.0	5.0	4.3	3.8	3.3	3.0
320	6.4	5.3	4.6	4.0	3.6	3.2
340	6.8	5.7	4.9	4.3	3.8	3.4
360	7.2	6.0	5.1	4.5	4.0	3.6
380	7.6	6.3	5.4	4.8	4.2	3.8
400	8.0	6.7	5.7	5.0	4.4	4.0
420	8.4	7.0	6.0	5.3	4.7	4.2
440	8.8	7.3	6.3	5.5	4.9	4.4
460	9.2	7.7	6.6	5.8	5.1	4.6
480	9.6	8.0	6.9	6.0	5.3	4.8
500	10.0	8.3	7.1	6.3	5.6	5.0

TIB3 and TIB4 provides the foundation to underpin your climbing. (Long climbs are essentially uphill time trials and so the type of training can be similar.)

If you are preparing for road racing, work on developing an explosive quality to your climbing to distance your rivals. Train by accelerating hard at TIB6 before settling into a steady TIB4 climbing rhythm. Using your power meter you will be able to see the impact of the explosive effort on your ability to hold a high constant power output afterwards.

Some riders find that they develop a climbing-specific fitness too. In other words, they are able to produce a higher power output when climbing than for the same duration on the flat. You can examine your climbing-specific fitness by making the same comparison with your power output. Find two sections of your training route where you can make a similar-length sustained hard effort, one section up a climb and the other on the flat. Ride these two sections as hard as you can and compare your average power output for each. Websites such as Strava and Map My Tracks can help you keep track of this by creating 'segments' where your time

Specific climbing fitness is something you should focus on if your event involves long hills, mountain climbs or technical climbs. (Photo courtesy of James Allen)

and average power output are automatically calculated every time you upload your data. Once you have marked out your segments you can easily see how your flat and climbing power compare, and whether either has improved from previous rides. In addition, looking at the performance of other riders on the same climb will give you an idea of your overall climbing fitness.

Specific climbing fitness is something you should focus on if your event involves long hills, mountain climbs or technical climbs. Long mountain climbs such as those found in the Alps and Pyrenees feature in most of the grand tours and many sportives. Riding on these climbs can involve going uphill for more than an hour at a time. Long climbs such as these are relentless as there are no chances for a break in your effort or rhythm. For many riders climbing like this is a different experience and it's one that

requires practice if you are to get used to it and do it well.

Gauging or pacing your effort is an important part of riding long climbs effectively. Once you have ridden a few long climbs with your power meter you should have a reasonable insight into the power output that you can expect to maintain. You can then use your power meter to establish an appropriate early pace at the beginning of long climbs and avoid the painful trap of starting too fast and fading while on the climb. Knowing yourself well is key, and you can easily outperform your rivals on a long climb by allowing them to sprint away at the bottom. Many riders, even experienced ones, make the mistake of starting the climb with a power output that is unsustainable for them. By gauging your effort carefully you will often find you can reel back and drop someone who has started faster than you. If they can start fast and stay away, then they deserve to finish in front of you!

The other way to boost your power-to-weight ratio and climb faster is to lose weight. Any weight lost counts, whether from your body, your bike or your clothing, enabling you to go uphill faster for the same power output. Therefore to climb really well you have to be both very fit and very light. This means that your power-to-weight ratio will be also very high. On a long mountain climb in the Tour de France, for example, the world's best riders can sustain a power to weight of around 6.5W/kg. For most riders, sustaining anything over 3W/kg takes considerable training and commitment. High power-to-weight ratios are achieved by a combination of being extremely powerful and very lean.

Sometimes when you lose weight you can also lose muscle mass and power output at the same time. Under these circumstances your weight loss is not necessarily beneficial. If your power-to-weight ratio is affected more by your loss in power output than your loss in weight, your climbing will get worse. Crash dieting and dehydration are examples where losing weight may not always pay off. In these situations the body weight you lose may be outweighed by your associated loss in climbing power output. As an example, consider a 100kg rider with a power output when climbing of 300W. This rider therefore has a power-to-weight ratio of 300 ÷ 100 = 3W/kg. After a rapid weight-loss programme the rider manages to lose 5kg but at a cost of 20W. Now you can calculate the rider's power-to-weight ratio as 280W ÷ 95kg = 2.95W/kg, which is lower than before. Far-fetched as this example may seem, I have several times had riders consult me because they are concerned about a mys-terious loss of power output in training or racing. Once they realized that the loss in power output was attributable to losing weight too quickly, they stopped trying to lose weight and their form returned.

Technical climbs are those you encounter off-road on your mountain bike, or where there are numerous changes in the gradient and pitch of the road. In these circumstances how you distribute your effort on the climb can make a notable difference to how well you climb. Practice and experience make a difference on climbs like these. Your learning is also faster if you can revisit the climb by examining the data from your power meter. Use your power meter data afterwards to examine both the gradient and the pattern with which you made your effort on the climb. Consider first your average power output for the climb, then look to see where the slowest and steepest parts of the climb were. If you have judged the climb well, your highest power output should be on the slowest (in other words the steepest) sections. Look for slow, steep sections where your power output is below average. These are regions of the climb where you could potentially improve by increasing your power output as the gradient kicks up. If you are able to repeat the climb, you can examine the effect of redistributing your power output, both in terms of your climbing speed and how your climbing power output changes. You will be surprised how many seconds you can save and how different a climb can feel when you redistribute your effort like this.

SPRINTING

Like riding fast in general, your sprinting prowess is mostly determined by the power

Sprinting is a highly skilled activity and to perform well you need not only the physical conditioning, but also great technical ability. (Radu Razvan/Shutterstock.com)

output you can produce and how aerodynamic you are. The higher your power output and the more aerodynamic you are, the faster your sprint will be. But remember that it is the aerodynamic drag for your sprinting position, not your general riding one, that counts.

During your sprint you are concerned only with producing the highest power output you can possibly sustain along the finishing straight. Typically this means your sprint takes only a few seconds. Your performance in such short, intense efforts is determined by your peak power output. Your peak power output is a measurement of the highest power output you can possibly produce. In a laboratory you would normally measure your peak power output from a six-second sprint. Your peak power output is usually achieved in the first three seconds of a sprint. After that, even in a six-second sprint, you will start to fatigue and your power output will drop away.

Fatigue is an inevitable consequence of any high-intensity muscular work. The more intense the work, the greater the fatigue you will experience. Thus the major determinants of your sprinting power output are your peak power output and how quickly you fatigue. It seems that training can help you really improve your peak power output, but in contrast your rate of fatigue does not necessarily respond so readily to training. This means that you should focus particularly on increasing your peak power output and your associated maximum sprinting speed.

Sprinting is a highly skilled activity and to perform it well you need not only appropriate physical conditioning but also great technical ability. In particular, you need excellent bike-handling skills, a lot of nerve and good timing. When sprinting you will not usually find a straight path to the finish. This is where your ability to read the sprint, handle your bike and manage your nerve will affect your performance. Finding and squeezing through small gaps between riders while sprinting hard is not for the fainthearted. Judging your effort correctly is also a skill. Start too early and you will fade before the line and be overtaken by your rivals who have benefitted from being led out by you. However, leave it too late to start your sprint and you will never reach the front of the race.

By examining your sprints with your power meter you can learn what kind of a sprinter you are. Broadly speaking, sprinters tend to be split into two types: the 'kickers' and the 'dragsters'. The kicker types are the riders who can produce an incredible acceleration in a short, sharp burst. The kickers tend to have very high peak power outputs.

In the sprint they will prefer to leave the final sprint late and burst across the line. The dragster sprinters are those who can produce and hold an impressive power output. The dragsters will tend to lead out a longer sprint at high speed, leaving other sprinters unable to get past. By looking at the shape of your power output when you sprint you can try and decide whether you are more of a 'kicker' or a 'dragster', and train and sprint accordingly.

Riders who are able to produce very impressive sprint power outputs tend to perform relatively poorly in more demanding aerobic and endurance events. Similarly, good time-trial riders often have a surprisingly low peak power output in a short sprint. In fact, some scientists have suggested that these attributes may be inversely related. This could mean that the better your time-trial ability the lower your sprinting performance and vice versa. When it comes to improving your sprinting this means it is not your aerobic fitness or VO_2max that you need to develop, but your sprint-specific power output.

Before examining sprint training in more detail, I should mention the critical roles of cadence and warming-up in sprinting. During endurance cycling, experience enables riders to find their optimal and comfortable cadence. Beyond this, keeping your cadence in the broad range of 80–110rpm does not seem to have a marked impact on your performance. When sprinting, however, cadence appears to have a much more obvious impact on your performance. Your best sprinting power output occurs at a specific cadence. Get this cadence wrong and your power output *will* suffer: a cadence that is too low or too high will mean that you cannot produce your true peak power output. The relationship between peak power output

MEASURE YOUR PEAK POWER OUTPUT

A power meter is an excellent tool with which to measure your sprint peak power output. Consistently hitting your peak power output takes a little practice, so do not be surprised if your results are not very consistent at first. After a little practice you should find that you can see the changes in peak power output associated with both your endurance and your sprint-specific training.

You should remember that your peak power output is quite sensitive to changes in your cadence and body temperature. This means that you should control your cadence by using the same stretch of road and gear ratio if you plan to compare your peak power output measures in the future. You should also ensure that you have had a thorough warm-up if you want to measure your true peak power output. You may also find that sprinting in or out of the saddle can make a difference to the power output you can generate, and therefore it is sensible to standardize this too. Unless you are specifically interested in your out-of-the-saddle sprint ability, I suggest that you standardize your test by measuring your peak power output in a seated sprint. Do make sure that your head unit or data logger is set to record your data at one-second intervals or less, otherwise you will not be able to see how your power output changes during your short six-second sprint.

To perform the test, warm-up thoroughly and then select a stretch of road that is fairly flat and quiet. You want to be able to make a maximum six-second effort without worrying about passing traffic. Ideally the road should not be too exposed to wind if you plan to do the test regularly and in different weather conditions. Depending on your power meter, you may need to switch on its head unit to ensure that it records as much of your sprint data as possible. Many power meters will not start recording until your cadence hits a minimum value of around 30 or 40rpm, though. I suggest that you select your lowest gear and make your sprint seated from as close to a standing start as you can manage.

The test itself is simply to accelerate as hard and aggressively as you possibly can for six seconds. If you do this on a flat road in your lowest gear you should find that you have revved out by the end of your sprint. Most power meter head units will automatically show you the highest power you produce during a ride, so you do not need to wait until you get home to find out how well you performed. However, it is instructive to download the file too, as by doing this you will be able to see the relationship between your cadence and your power output. After you have recorded a few sprints you will have a good idea of the cadence at which you produce your peak power output. Typically your peak power output will occur at an optimal cadence of between 100 and 120rpm.

and cadence is shown in Figure 12. However, with a power meter your optimal cadence is easy to find. You just need to sprint at different cadences and see where your highest power output occurs. You can do this by selecting different gears for your sprints. Alternatively, see the box on measuring your peak power output. For most riders, optimal cadence for peak power output tends to occur between 100 and 130rpm.

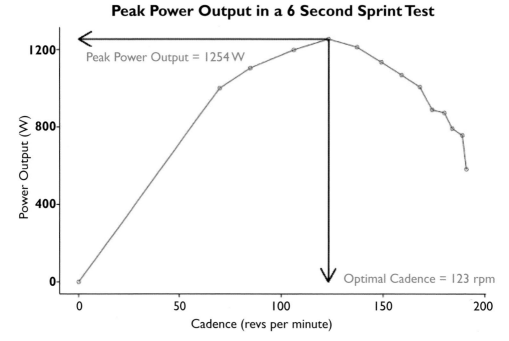

Fig. 12 **Peak power output in a six-second sprint test.**

Warm-up can have quite a noticeable effect on your peak power output. The effect seems much more obvious on sprint peak power output than it does on endurance performance. The biological reason for the effects of warm-up are well established. Heating your muscles with hot pads rather than a warm-up exercise can increase the sprint peak power output you are capable of producing.

In a recent study sports scientists in Glasgow heated the legs of eight riders with hot water and heated blankets before getting them to sprint. The blankets raised the riders' muscle temperature by almost 10 per cent and as a result increased their peak power output by more than 20 per cent. For this reason British Cycling developed shorts with heating pads built into them for the track team's riders at the London Olympic Games in 2012. These shorts (inevitably

called 'hot pants') meant the GB riders could warm-up more easily before competition. They could also stay warmer during the pause that inevitably occurs before the start of their race.

Warm-up exercises are both the simplest and most effective way to increase the temperature of your muscles, so you do not need to worry about using heat pads or blankets. The most important thing is that you are aware of the benefits of a thorough warm-up before you start training or testing your sprint peak power output.

Training to improve your peak power output primarily requires you to perform maximum very high-intensity efforts. Focus on TIB7 training sessions in your programme. Your peak power output is achieved by a combination of high pedal forces and high cadence. Therefore you can look for ways to train each of these aspects separately as well as together. To train at high pedal forces you can use a lower cadence or increase the resistance you are pedalling against. To provide lower cadences, simply use a larger gear. To provide really low cadences and a high pedal force, use the largest gear you have got from a standing start. To increase the pedal force even more, perform your efforts going uphill. By manipulating your cycling conditions you can create a situation on your bike where the forces are so great that you can hardly turn the pedals. Here you are doing strength training without even leaving your bike.

The other part of producing a high peak power is by increasing your cadence. To do this you need to learn to pedal fast – really fast. This is not like trying to learn to pedal smoothly in a time trial. Instead, you are trying to teach your body to improve the co-ordination of your maximum pedalling and to increase your fastest possible cadence. To do this you can reverse the principles for creating high forces. Now you want to train in a lower gear to make it easy to pedal quickly. You can even practise your high-cadence sprints on a very slight downhill gradient. You should quickly find yourself in a situation where it is your leg speed that is limiting how fast you pedal and not the power output that you are producing. By performing repeated sprints and systematically manipulating the condition for these sprints, you should start to see improvements in your sprint peak power output.

As this is a highly skilled activity and your normal sprints and low-cadence sprints are very fatiguing, you should break your training into repeated repetitions and sets of efforts. A repetition is a single sprint effort. A set may consist of three to six single sprints that you group together before taking a longer rest period. As an example,

you might perform 3 × 100-metre sprints at close to your optimal cadence and just freewheel between each of the sprints. After this set you should then take a longer recovery (for example six minutes) before repeating the set again. Depending on your fitness, you might perform between two and five sets (in other words six to fifteen sprints in total). In addition to altering the number of repetitions and sets, you can also change the length of each sprint. Sometimes you should train for very short, explosive efforts. This is akin to your final lunge for the finish line. These might be 50 to 100 metres long. On other occasions you might perform repetitions of single sprints that are much longer, perhaps 300 metres long. Note that to improve your sprinting you do not want to train much beyond 300 metres, as otherwise there is a risk that the fitness benefits may not be as relevant to your sprinting ability.

For the same reasons, you should also make sure that the power output you are producing is always near the top of your TIB7 range. In general you are trying to reproduce your best efforts in these training sessions. The emphasis of your training should be on maintaining a high-quality effort. This means you should allow yourself sufficient rest between sprint efforts that you can recover fully and work at or close to 100 per cent of your peak power output. Once you feel you are starting to fatigue substantially and the quality of your efforts is deteriorating, it is time to stop. You will not be able to improve your peak power output by making half-hearted efforts that are not close to your maximum.

The extent to which you focus on your sprints in training depends upon the type of events you plan to ride (and sprint in). If you are an endurance road rider training your final race sprint, you must have the endurance and aerobic fitness to get you to the finish. In order to use your sprint to perform well, you have to be in a race position worth sprinting from. Therefore your primary training focus should be on your overall road-racing fitness until you are confident that your fitness enables you to get to the end of the race in a competitive position. If you are more interested in shorter track races, or perhaps the track sprint itself, then you can afford to specialize and focus on your sprint training to a much greater extent.

Your sprinting power comes from the size of your muscles. The larger your muscles, the more force you can produce on the pedals and the faster you will go on your bike. On the flat, because your bike carries your weight there is little penalty to you for being bigger and heavier. In a sprint this extra size enables you to produce more power and makes you a better sprinter. But once you introduce hills into the equation the situation changes markedly. Here the extra weight of a bulky sprinter's muscles is really slowed by the pull of gravity. This is why it is very unusual to find top riders who excel both in the mountains and in the final sprint. Even if you are not an elite rider you may have to decide where on this continuum you want to position yourself and train accordingly.

TIME TRIALS

The key determinants of performance in a time trial are your sustainable power output and your aerodynamic drag. The higher your sustainable power output, or the lower your aerodynamic drag, the faster your race performance will be.

To excel in time trials you must develop your ability to sustain a high power output for the duration of the race. The best time-trial riders have a very high level of aerobic fitness in terms of their VO_2max and, in particular, the percentage of this that they can sustain for a race. If you want to go fast in a time trial you will also need to fine-tune your fitness so that you can adapt to sustain a very high percentage of your maximum minute power output.

Many years ago, in a classic scientific study, Professor Ed Coyle from the University of Texas compared the laboratory performance of two groups of riders in the laboratory. For both groups of riders the VO_2max was almost identical. At race pace the picture was quite different though. Despite having similar maximum levels of fitness, one group showed marked signs of stress at TIB4, with elevated blood lactate levels. In contrast the other group appeared to be still quite comfortable. Unsurprisingly, the comfortable group easily outperformed the stressed group by being able to ride twice as long in a time-to-exhaustion trial. This study tells us that it is not simply your VO_2max or maximum minute power output that dictates how well you perform. You also need to consider how well you can sustain a high percentage of your maximum. If you want to be good at time trials you not only need a high maximum but to be comfortable sustaining a high percentage of your maximum. The reassuring news from the Texas study was that ability to sustain a high percentage seemed to correspond with the group's cycle training history. This suggests that this aspect of your fitness, so critical to time-trial performance, is trainable.

To prepare for time trials specifically you should train first to develop a high level of aerobic and endurance fitness before developing the ability to sustain a high percentage of this fitness for the duration of the time trial. The approach for developing your aerobic and endurance fitness I have covered already; it is essentially the same whether you plan to ride the road, time trials, mountain bike, cross country or sportives. But to summarize again, your training focus will be on building fitness with brisk TIB2 and TIB3 endurance rides. As most time trials tend to be between ten and fifty miles long, you may find that you do not need to perform the longer training sessions typical of the road and sportive riders. If you tend to focus mostly on the shorter distance time trials, TIB2 and TIB3 sessions of up to three hours should be perfectly sufficient; this will still take your training rides considerably beyond race distance.

The key difference for you in comparison with riders who do not focus on the time trial is the training to increase the power output you can sustain in a race. A useful starting point for this kind of training is to measure the power output you can average for a time trial. Ideally you should do this in an actual race. If you are preparing for a specific time trial, use your time-trial bike and ride the same or a similar course to the race for which you are preparing. If you are the curious type, you may want to perform the maximum test (described earlier) so that you can see what percentage of your maximum you race at. However, for the purposes of training you do not need to know your maximum, only the power output you can currently maintain in a time trial.

Next you need to set about incrementing your time-trial power output. You set about this in two ways, by both 'pushing' and 'pulling' your time-trial power output higher. The pushing training involves training sessions that are at or very close to your time-trial power output. In these training sessions you are trying to train at a power output just below your time-trial power output but for longer. These will be high TIB3 or low TIB4 sessions where you maintain the same type of effort as in a time-trial. Because you are deliberately training slightly below your time-trial intensity, you should be able to accumulate considerable training time at close to your race pace. The aim of these sessions is to enable you to feel increasingly comfortable making this kind of effort at just below race pace. As you begin to feel the benefits of this training you should find that you are able to ride closer to your race power output. Now, like the comfortable group in the Texas study, riding at (the bottom of) TIB4 should feel less stressful and something you can keep going for longer.

The pulling training is focused on teaching your body to ride at a new, higher power output. We are all creatures of habit. This is especially true when it comes to training and racing. The research and analysis on training that I have done shows that we will tend to adhere to remarkably similar training patterns, speeds and power outputs even over the course of a whole year. I have regularly analysed training programmes, where despite some completely new training sessions being introduced, the new, modified programme was more similar than dissimilar to its predecessor. The philosophy you need to adopt is that in order to *change* your race speed you need to *change* the training that underpins it.

Once again, the good news is that by using a power meter this type of session becomes relatively simple to implement. I should perhaps add that it is physically challenging to perform, but it is simple to plan! In essence your training plan is to *change* your training power output by purposefully adopting a higher one. As you have already determined your typical time-trial power output, you can easily identify a target power output for your training session that is higher than you currently produce in a time trial. During your training session, you are going to try and spend time riding at this new target power output above the your previous time-trial level. With a target set like this your motivational drive to complete the session will be high, as you know exactly why you are attempting the session. Because your target power output is deliberately above your current time-trial power output, it is immediately obvious that you will not be able to maintain it for very long. This means that you will have to keep recovering from your efforts at the target power output by performing intervals. You want riding at this new power output to become a habit so you will need to do as many as possible. Therefore the structure of the session is to perform short intervals of around one minute at your target power output, then take a short recovery of the same one-minute duration and repeat. As the efforts are short and you get a recovery, you can repeat again and again and again. In fact you can repeat the effort so often that it almost starts to become a new habit!

To do lots of efforts you need to complete a reasonable length ride. Oscillating between TIB1 and TIB4 like this makes for challenging training sessions, even with the recovery periods. Typically, you should perform these sessions for between forty and eighty minutes. Less than forty minutes will not really be habit forming. Longer than eighty minutes may not be sustainable and you risk sliding back to your normal race power output. Although you do not have to be super fresh to perform these intervals, they are tiring both physically and mentally. Do not plan to do anything particularly taxing afterwards. As your fitness improves, especially if you are working towards a specific target power output, you can first increase the interval period (for example to two minutes). Then, if you are really going well in training, try reducing your recovery period to thirty seconds. But if you can get this close to your target power output, maybe you are ready to change or increment your training again. The next evolution of this strategy is to reduce the length of your training session to a more conventional TIB4 duration and perform longer time-trial type intervals.

Performing longer extended intervals or continuous time-trial efforts is a critical part of your overall race preparation. This is because the skill of measuring or pacing your effort over the course of a race has important physiological and psychological bases. From a physiological perspective you are also training your body to be as efficient as possible. You aim to sustain as high a power output as possible over an extended period of time in your racing position. This takes practice to perform well. For this type of training you are using TIB4 sessions. You can do this in intervals and sustained efforts, but keep the intervals to at least five minutes in length. This is because you are learning to make sustained efforts. Shorter intervals, unless they have a very short recovery, will not provide you with the same type of training overload. When first making this type of effort, fifteen minutes or 3 × 5-minute intervals is sufficient. As you become used to sustaining this type of effort and coping with the mounting discomfort, increment the length of the session until you can manage around thirty minutes or 6 × 5 minutes. Try to maintain the same power output as you extend the length of your sessions. Where you are performing these TIB4 sessions as intervals, keep your recovery periods quite short. This is to maintain the sensations and stress of making a sustained effort. Around a minute or two for recovery between intervals is about right. If you are chasing a new higher power output then you may need to extend your recovery a little in order to maintain the power output.

From a psychological perspective these types of effort take considerable concentration and motivation against a backdrop of increasing fatigue. Therefore accustoming yourself to making and sustaining these efforts is a very important part of your training process. Whilst your ability to sustain a high power output is largely determined by your physiological capabilities, recent research from Professor Sam Marcora in our endurance research group has highlighted the critical role played by the brain too. During time-trial efforts, part of the fatigue you experience will be specific to the brain. It's called mental fatigue. One of the ways in which you can notice the effects of mental fatigue is that your perception of effort increases. This means that you will experience an increase in how hard it feels to maintain a constant power output. This increase in your perceived exertion is related to the mental cost associated with your physical effort. In a neat experiment, Professor Marcora showed that increased mental fatigue is associated with a reduced time-trial performance. The study participants had to complete a mentally fatiguing task before a time trial on two occasions. On one occasion the task was particularly demanding,

requiring high concentration. The time trial following the demanding mental task was 6 per cent worse and the participants' perception of effort was 9 per cent higher than for the other time trial. Everyone seems to be susceptible to the effects of this mental fatigue on performance, but some early research findings from our laboratory suggest that your training may reduce its impact on performance. Therefore regard your TIB4 training as both physical and mental training.

Finally, it is important that you perform some of your training in your racing position, as this is often different from the position on your standard road bike. Make your TIB4 sessions specific to the race, using the same bike, riding position and type of roads where possible. If you don't do this you may find that you are unable to produce or sustain the power output that you would expect when riding on your time-trial bike or in your time-trial position. Bear in mind too that there can be a need to compromise between a faster, more aerodynamic position and a slower, less aerodynamic one that is more powerful or sustainable. By training with your power meter in your time-trial position you can compare your power output when riding in both positions. Often riders report that they prefer to race in a less aerodynamic but more powerful and sustainable position.

SPORTIVE OR CENTURY RIDES

Sportives have grown enormously in popularity in recent years. Consequently, there are quite a number of these events with varying levels of difficulty in which you can take part. Some of the toughest sportives follow the same or similar routes as the professional riders in top races. These rides can present a very challenging route even for a well-trained cyclist. Using a power meter in preparation for and during a sportive will allow you to assess the demands of the event, guide and track your training for the event, and help you pace your effort on the day.

One of the challenges of the big sportives on a tough route is that it can be a journey into the unknown. If you are not familiar with the route and have not ridden the kind of terrain featured for that event it can be very hard to know what to expect and prepare for. However, with a little research on the Internet and armed with your own power meter, you can prepare knowing exactly how challenging the route is likely to be. In addition, you can also assess what kind of condition you need to be in to complete the challenge and how much training is required to get you in shape.

As with the other cycling events, sportive success is built on a foundation of aerobic and endurance training. Indeed for many riders a regular diet of TIB2 and TIB3 training is the main training that is required for a sportive. You do not need to specialize in your training, particularly as you are largely riding against yourself rather than others. As with all training programme planning, it is still worth starting by thinking about your goals. Sportives and the preparation for them can be completed largely for enjoyment and this can easily be reflected in your goal. Remember the process is about setting goals that specify where you would like to be in your training before the event. In this instance you may decide that chasing a particular level of 'performance' or time is not for you. You can reflect this by setting yourself training goals that you will find fun and challenging. For example, you may enjoy completing certain training routes or climbs. You could specify an average power output for the ride or a particular segment of the ride. However, if you have a particular level of performance in mind for the sportive, or if the route and/ or time limit are likely to be particularly challenging for you, then you will need to set yourself goals that are more focused on reaching a specific level of fitness.

Your first step is to determine what information on the sportive event is already available. You are looking for information that will help you assess the demands or challenges of the event. If it is a particularly challenging route consider a recce or fact-finding trip. This recce may be on the actual route. If the event is too far away to use the actual route, perhaps you can arrange a ride or two somewhere nearer that has similar terrain. However, if it is a big event or uses an iconic route or roads, there is a good chance that most of the information you need is already available somewhere on the Internet. Ideally, you are looking for a route map with a profile and an associated power meter trace from someone who has ridden the route. Even without the power meter file you can make some useful estimates from a map and route profile. First look at the length of the event and any time limits that the organizers have imposed. This will tell you the minimum speed you need to average. Look at how this speed compares with your usual training rides. If there is a notable difference you may need to work quite hard on improving your aerobic fitness in order to sustain the speed required.

Next consider the route profile and how this might impact on the demands of the event. The simplest way is to consider the length of the climbs and the total metres of climbing involved. Look at how the amount of climbing compares with some of your previous rides. If there is a big difference you should plan on including some particularly hilly routes in your preparation. Refer back to the earlier section on climbing for more details about this. You can also see if you can find any power meter data relating to the route, or part of it. There are a number of websites where riders upload their data and allow it to be shared, such as Garmin, Strava and Map My Tracks. If the sportive organizers have not provided an example on their website, it is worth searching on these sites to see if you can find something. By looking at other riders' power output profile for the ride in conjunction with their speed, you will get a feel for the kind of goal you need to set for yourself in training. This does not have to be an exact science; you are simply trying to estimate the approximate nature of the challenge that you are preparing to complete.

Write down your observations from this research. Now you can use this information to establish some specific training goals for yourself. Set yourself a training goal or goals that when completed before the event will give you confidence that you are fit for your target sportive or century ride. These could be based on average power output targets for certain length rides or segments of the ride. For example, you could have a goal to average 160W for a hilly four-hour ride and to average 190W for particular climbs on that route. If you complete this goal three weekends before the sportive you can feel confident that you are ready for the event itself. Your training leading up to the sportive can be based around TIB2 and TIB3 sessions where you aim to average 160W, or to average 190W on less challenging hills.

MTB

Performing well in MTB races requires above-average aerobic fitness and also a good power-to-weight ratio. (See the earlier climbing section for details about your power-to-weight ratio and how to calculate it.) Off-road riding typically involves a lot of climbing and acceleration. As I have discussed previously in this chapter, your body weight creates a significant penalty when climbing and accelerating. It is no accident that some of the best MTB riders can transition to road racing and make excellent climbers. In recent years there has been a trend in MTB racing toward faster and more technical 'park' style racing and away from 'mountain' style courses. Nonetheless, the amount of climbing in these races can be deceptive; it is just that this climbing may take the form of many short 'power' ascents rather than sustained 'tempo' climbing. In addition, these park courses do require you to produce acceleration out of corners, after slower sections and to overtake lagging riders. This can be every bit as demanding as long, challenging climbs. For these reasons MTB riders need excellent all-round fitness. This all-round fitness is not just in terms of VO_2max and sprint fitness, but also on- and off-bike conditioning too.

Off-road riders usually do quite a lot of their training on the road. There are two reasons for this. First, off-road riding slows your recovery as riding off-road is physically much more demanding, with bumpy surfaces creating vibration and your bike juddering and jarring your body as you pedal. This extra stress also has an impact on your power meter. There is much less power meter data available for mountain bike riding. This paucity of data is partly due to the different specification of cranks and

Performing well in MTB races requires above average aerobic fitness and also a good power to weight ratio.

hubs that MTBs typically use, which makes it harder to find and fit power meters. However, the main reason is that when they are fitted power meters tend not to be as reliable due to the added stress of riding off-road. Therefore, think carefully before you invest in your power meter for off-road riding. You will benefit from being one of few riders able to collect significant amounts of off-road data, but you need to pick a power meter that you judge to be robust as no other cycling discipline subjects its equipment to such abuse.

The second reason that you may need more recovery after riding off-road is due to the difficulty of controlling your power output. When you ride off-road the changes in riding surface and gradient necessitate big variations in your power output. This results in marked differences in your power output profile for road and off-road rides. If you already have a power meter on your MTB, take a moment to compare files or segments from riding on and off-road. Figure 13 shows power data for an elite MTB rider training off-road in preparation

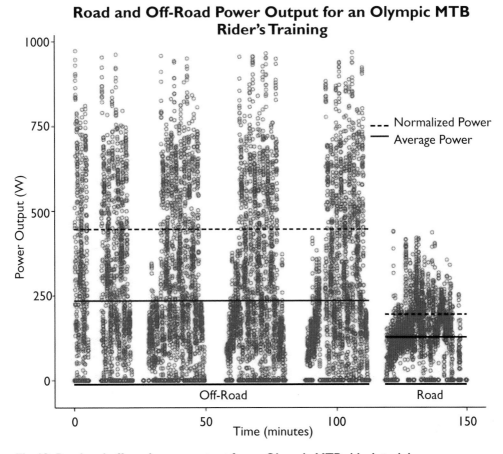

Fig. 13 Road and off-road power output for an Olympic MTB rider's training.

for an Olympic Games. You can easily see that off-road riding requires much larger variations in power output than road riding. Consequently, when you train off-road you will spend little time riding at a consistent work rate. Therefore if you are an MTB rider your road-based training provides your core aerobic and endurance training. This road-based training is similar to that for a road race or a reasonable-length time trial. To establish your basic aerobic and endurance fitness you can follow a similar approach to that set out in the road race and time trial sections earlier in this chapter.

But although you race as hard as you can from start to finish in both a time trial and an MTB race, the other demands are quite different. The highly variable nature of the MTB race means you need to include some much more varied riding in your training too.

When you are riding off-road, being able to increase your power output quickly will enable you to race faster over the slower sections of an MTB course. This is not the kind of effort that a time-trial rider normally has to make. Therefore, regularly include repeated short intervals in TIB5 and

TIB6 in your training programme. As you approach your main off-road races, make your on-road TIB4 sessions more specific by riding on your MTB on the road but with road wheels.

With the loose surface it seems that MTB riders pedal differently when they ride off-road. On the road you can stamp on your pedals to increase your power output. When riding off-road you have to apply your pedal forces more smoothly and actively pedal in circles at high power outputs. To maintain this pedalling style and develop excellent technical skills, it is important that you incorporate some off-road TIB4 sessions into your programme. Mix up the gradient for these sessions so that your TIB4 race-paced efforts include both technical paths and non-technical climbs of different gradients. Inexperienced riders often make the mistake of not doing enough fast off-road riding. Riding slowly off-road will not provide you with the opportunity to develop an appropriate pedalling style, nor will it allow you to fine-tune your technical skills.

In MTB races you will often produce efforts close to your peak power output. You do this when the course rises up sharply, after you exit a slow corner or to overtake a slower rider after a bottleneck. Your peak power output is developed in TIB7 sessions. You can train for these situations by making short efforts (five to thirty seconds) with a reasonable recovery between efforts (at least three minutes). Like sprint training you need to be well warmed-up and not feeling tired to make these sessions count. Unlike sprint training you should really mix up the gears that you are in when making these efforts. Cover the range from big over-geared, low-cadence, high-force efforts to small-gear, high-cadence, low-force sprints.

When you race off-road you do not always have full control over your cadence and gear selection, so you need to train to be able to produce a high power output regardless of your situation.

TRIATHLON

The bike section of the triathlon is both similar and different to other types of cycling event in the challenges it presents. Similar to other events is your need to cycle as fast as possible in order to match or beat your rivals. Where the triathlon is different is that you have to be able to run fast after you have finished the cycling section. Typically the cycling section is the longest part of the race, both in terms of distance and time taken to complete it. In other words it presents the greatest opportunity for you to gain, or to lose, time on your competitors during the triathlon. Therefore you can reflect this in the time you spend cycling in preparation for a triathlon. However, there are factors that you should consider that may mitigate somewhat against this emphasis on cycling. First (and despite this book's focus on cycle training), it is important to note that your triathlon race is concluded with your running performance. Second, drafting in elite triathlon races provides the means to save considerable energy during the cycling leg, or to race faster than you could manage alone. The upshot of both factors is that those races that feature bunches or groups of triathletes racing together should be prepared for differently. If you are preparing for a race where drafting is allowed, you should think about placing increased emphasis on your run training. This is because unless you are exceptionally strong in the cycling section you should find yourself finishing with a group. In addition to an increased focus on running, your cycle training must also have a different focus as you are preparing for bunch rather than lone riding. Consequently, as an elite triathlete your training will follow more closely that of a road rider, rather than a time trialist. Having noted this, however, I will focus the rest of this section on preparing for the cycling section of triathlons where drafting or pacing is not allowed.

Although the bike leg is the longest part of the race, it is likely that at the end of this section there will still be other athletes near you. Consequently, your result is likely to be determined by your ability to run off the bike. Your bike training should be designed to allow you to run as well as possible. Train with your power meter to try to extract the maximum benefit from each cycle session whilst minimizing its impact on your running. For example, recent research from the University of Loughborough compared the impact of constant and variable intensity cycling on subsequent running performance. The researchers found that variable intensity cycling has a more noticeable impact on subsequent running performance. The implication of this is that where appropriate your training should focus on sustaining high and even intensity efforts. However, for hilly races you should vary your effort to pace your race most effectively. Accordingly, you will need to prepare differently to flat races, in which you can sustain a consistent effort. Training with your power meter will enable you to monitor how hard you can afford to push on the climbs, before it really starts to impact on your run. For flat races you can use your power meter to identify the maximum even-paced effort you can sustain.

Overall, your broad training strategy for Triathlon should follow the same as outlined

in the time trial section. A good aerobic and endurance base fitness is particularly important for Triathlon. This is because it provides a foundation not only for your cycling but also your swimming and running too. The demand of preparing for three disciplines means that you will tend to stress your body more with your overall training load in comparison with someone who trains for only one. Your endurance training provides the conditioning necessary to be able to sustain this higher training load as it accumulates across three disciplines and recover quickly for the next session. It is a good idea to put particular emphasis on using your bike training, rather than the more stressful swimming and running sessions, to build aerobic and endurance fitness where you can. As a consequence you may find that you need to polarize your training more than other cyclists. This polarization means that your training emphasises the more extreme training intensities (i.e. TIB2 and TIB5), rather more than those in the middle (TIB3 and TIB4).

With three disciplines to train, you need to spend your training time wisely. You still need to get the right balance between training and recovery whilst maintaining your run and swim training alongside your bike riding. As a consequence you should expect your overall bike training volume to be somewhat less than someone who is focused solely on cycling. One of the ways you can compensate for training a little less is by training a little harder on your bike instead. This is consistent with trying to polarize your training as discussed above. When using TIBs in training, target the shorter end of the time range. Then you can compensate for the shorter duration by using your power meter to focus your effort on training in the upper part of your

TIB. For example, TIB3 sessions are typically 45 to 90 minutes, so aim for the lower end of this range, but try to keep your average power output above the TIB target mid-point for your ride. Ultimately you are trying to complete the minimum cycling training you need to get fit, whilst maximizing the benefits you can achieve from each session. If you are relatively inexperienced or training for Olympic triathlon you may be able to make good progress with only a couple of rides a week. However, as you become more experienced, or if you are planning on tackling Ironman distances, you will need to boost both your training duration and frequency to reflect this.

Your bike training for the Triathlon should look similar to that of a time trial rider in principle. You will largely focus on developing good aerobic and endurance fitness. Your fitness will be built on a regular diet of TIB2 and TIB3 rides. As with road riders, your aim is to build aerobic and endurance fitness base to make you as fast as possible. In addition to your core endurance fitness you need to be able to sustain a high power output over a period of time just like a time trial rider. This type of fitness is created with sustained TIB4 training sessions, particularly for longer distance triathlons. If you are only focusing on shorter races up to Olympic distance, then you may find TIB5 more appropriate for your race specific training. Unless you are competing in hilly or bunch races, you will not need to produce short bursts of very high power output when racing. Therefore you do not need to regularly include efforts of this nature such as repeated TIB6 intervals. However, you may find that the added 'bite' provided from the shock of short sharp intervals gives all your training a lift. Therefore do look to include these sessions on occasion. Several TIB6 sessions performed in the final few weeks can contribute usefully and help you to hit peak form. In general training for Triathlon you do not need to be too concerned about TIB7 training. This type of training would only tend to be relevant for elite triathletes working closely with a coach.

CHAPTER TEN

MONITORING
YOUR TRAINING

Once you have completed each training session it is time to make sense of the data that you have generated and collected. To do this there is a range of software and websites that will help you (see the box on 'Software and Websites' in Chapter 2 for more information). Some of these options offer basic ways of looking at the details of the ride you have just completed. Others enable you to perform advanced analysis of your power meter data and it would require a separate book to learn how to use them. Here I will cover the basics. If you feel comfortable with this and are curious to extend your analysis then do take a look at some of the more advanced tools that are available. As the software and websites change regularly I have included details of them on my website at www.trainingwith-powermeters.co.uk.

When you first look at the details uploaded from a training ride you can easily feel overwhelmed by data. Over time you will become more familiar with your data and aspects of your ride that you like to pick out in your software or on a website. Indeed I often find that there are usually two or three different things that I look for and these are easier to find by using *different* websites. Therefore it is worth exploring

different options to see what works for you. A second advantage of using more than one website is that you have a backup of your training data in more than one place should something happen to your computer or one of the websites that you normally rely on.

One of the first things you will notice with your training data is the overall pattern of the ride. Unless you have been training indoors on a turbo, your power output varies a lot. There will be periods where your power output drops to 0W as you freewheel downhill. At the other extreme you can have spikes in your power output up to several hundred watts as you accelerate hard or go up a steep climb. Often this variation in your power output can obscure the overall pattern in your ride. To deal with this issue most software programs allow you to smooth your data so that you can choose the level of detail with which your ride is shown. In contrast most websites do not offer this option but set what they feel is the most appropriate for their users. If you prefer the way your power data look on a particular website then the smoothing they use could be a reason to use it. But being able to control this is one of the benefits of using your own software.

When you start looking at the data analysis from your ride, you will be shown your average power output for the whole ride. This is one of the most obvious metrics to look at and to track over time. Perhaps you averaged 140W in your most recent ride. As you get fitter you will see this average power output progressing to higher values. When this happens you will know that your training is being effective. At the upper end elite riders can average well over 300W for several hours in a hard race. Surprisingly few websites or programs make it easy to plot the changes in your average power output from ride to ride. Therefore you may find it useful to keep a note of your ride averages in a separate spreadsheet so that you can keep your own check on how your training progresses.

The next thing that you may want to look at is your power output for specific parts of the ride. Often the average power output will not give you the whole picture, perhaps because you have not tried to keep a steady tempo throughout. Instead you may have planned to use more than one TIB and therefore you want to look at the segments where you were in the higher TIB. With some power meters like the SRM it is easy to place a marker on your file as you begin and end the effort. This is then shown by the software as a selected region on your ride. This is great for interval sessions as you can quickly and easily check your performance in each effort, often before even downloading your power meter. Some devices and websites do not offer this facility, however. This is where websites that allow you to create and track separate segments on your ride are very helpful. The Strava website was one of the first to offer this facility, although others such as Map My Tracks provide it too. It means that once you have created or iden-

tified where the segments are on your route, you only have to concentrate on riding hard for that relevant segment. After your ride the website will sift through your data as you upload it and automatically find and display your performance in each segment. This can make planning a ride with a series of efforts a breeze once you know where the segments are or have added your own. It does mean that you have to ride with a device that has GPS as well as a power meter, though, as the website needs this data to work out which segments you have ridden.

Having looked at the pattern of your whole ride and perhaps different segments within it, you should also think about monitoring your training as part of your overall strategy. You are looking to determine whether you met your training objectives. Or, to put it another way, did you actually train in the TIB(s) as you planned? All software and several websites allow you specify the power output for each of your TIBs as part of your user profile (although some websites charge for this facility). This means that after you have uploaded your training data you may be able to see both the absolute intensity of your ride (watts) and the relative intensity as time in each of your personal TIBs. If your training session (or a segment of it) was intended to be in TIB3, for example, is this reflected in your actual training data? Your power output can vary between different TIBs even during a consistent effort, so do not expect to manage 100 per cent of your ride within your target TIB. Rather, look to see if your average power output is where you would expect. As I mentioned previously, research has shown that athletes deviate significantly from the programmes their coaches intended. Look for this possibility regularly and make necessary adjustments, either to your plan or your training rides, as soon as it occurs.

If you have a set goal to increment your average power output for a particular ride, your post-ride analysis is when the preparation for the next ride begins. In your post-ride analysis make a note of your average power output for the ride or segment that your goal is based around. Consider how your actual power output compares with your ultimate goal and also how long you have left to achieve your goal. With this information you can set your next incremental target by simple interpolation. For example, imagine your goal is to average 215W for a segment with a deadline of three weeks' time. When you download your power meter you find you have just averaged 200W for your target segment. Therefore, to find the extra 15W you aim to increase your segments by 5W per week in your successive rides. In this way you can reach your incremental goals and ensure progression in your training.

Be careful how you pursue this method, however, as you should not turn *every* training ride into a battle with your average power output. The simplest strategy is to have just one or two sessions per week that are incremented in this way. Identify one area of fitness or TIB that you are focusing on in that particular training block. For example, early in your preparation you may be focused on developing endurance in long rides at TIB2 and TIB3, and so you could increment one of these. Later in the year perhaps you are trying to improve your short time-trial or hill-climb segments instead. The rest of your training rides can still be monitored and checked to see if they are on plan but without setting the same demanding incremental goals. Trying to increment your training too fast or in

more than one area is the classic recipe for over training.

Each time you complete a training block take the opportunity to look at the longer-term trends in your power meter data. You are looking for signs that your fitness is responding to the training you are completing. The most obvious sign is an increase in your average training power output, either for your overall sessions or for your favourite segments. Ideally you should be able to see this as a regular progressive increase in your average power output, possibly over the current training block but more usually over several training blocks. Once your increment in average power output reaches 10–15W you should also be able to see changes in the speed of your training sessions and in your cardiovascular response too. Ultimately, you are training to be able to cycle faster. With a 15W increase in your average power output you should be able to see an obvious increase in the speed of your training sessions too. Changes of this magnitude are also likely to be visible in your underlying physiology. This improved aerobic fitness will reduce your cardiovascular strain and you should be able to see your power output has increased for a given heart rate. If you record your session RPE after each training ride, you should also find that your session RPE has reduced for a given average power output.

Because of the high variation in power output during your training rides, you may not be able to spot your signs of improvement easily. One way you can help make changes more visible and learn a little more about your responses is by completing regular standardized rides. During the competitive season or if you have very limited time to train this may not be practical. But wintertime can provide an obvious opportunity to do this, especially if you

POWER METER HEAD UNITS

In recent years power meters have adopted wireless technology to transmit your data to its head unit or data-logging device. Two popular protocols have emerged for doing this: these are Bluetooth and ANT+. This has the benefit that it is now possible to 'mix and match' power meters and data-logging devices. Indeed, some power meter manufacturers such as Stages have chosen not to produce a head unit at all but to ensure their power meter can talk to a range of other manufacturers' data-logging devices.

Ultimately it is your data-logging device that dictates the ease with which you can save and download your data. This means that you do not necessarily have to change your power meter to take advantage of a different method of saving or downloading your power meter data. It also means that when choosing your head unit or data-logging device you can ensure it offers the features you want in terms of data storage, data download, and software and website compatibility for your data analysis.

train indoors. The most standardized way to complete a ride is indoors on a static trainer, but with a little thought you could potentially do something similar outdoors. Your aim is to provide yourself with the same challenge every time you perform your standardized ride. Then any changes you observe are likely to be due to differences in your fitness. The most obvious way of performing a standardized ride is to hold a constant power output for a set period of time. The power output you choose needs to be sufficiently stressful that any changes in fitness become apparent. If you pick a low power output it will feel easy every time and you will not learn anything from this. I would suggest that your power output should correspond to near the top of TIB3 or the bottom of TIB4. Once you have identified a power output, keep this the same for every ride thereafter. The length of the ride needs to be enough for your body to reach a steady state. Prolonging it beyond this provides little further benefit, so ten minutes should be sufficient. If you are a high-performance athlete you may prefer twenty minutes including a warm-up. During the ride try to keep everything as consistent as possible and record your heart rate and session RPE. If you can, record your breathing rate towards the end of the time too, by counting the number of breaths you take over a minute. Your first ride will not tell you very much but over a period of time you should be able to see changes in your responses as your fitness varies. An interesting alternative approach is to switch the test round and ride to a constant heart rate rather than power output. In this way you can chart how your power output varies from test to test instead.

TRAINING DIARY

In addition to saving the data from your power meter, it can be useful to keep a training diary. If you are using a power meter regularly it is worth looking at the software or website you use to see if it offers options to do this. However, a paper-based training diary will also do the job just as effectively.

In your diary it is useful to keep a few brief notes on each training ride. Your training diary information is something that you are likely to look back on only occasionally, but when you do look at it you are probably looking for a specific reason. The reason is usually either to remember how you prepared for an event so you can repeat it, or because something has gone wrong and you are trying to work out why or what to do about it. Therefore it is useful if you have regular diary entries that summarize the key bits of information from your ride.

I suggest you keep each entry very short but outline the route and how your ride felt, in addition to any other statistics or information that you are likely to be interested in, such as an average power, heart rate and training distance and time. A simple way of recording how you felt is to use Borg's sessional rating of perceived exertion (RPE). The scale for this is provided in Table 2 alongside the description of your TIBs. The aim of the diary is to give a little extra background or context to each of your power meter training files.

MAINTENANCE PROGRAMME

Your training programme is focused on specifying what you intend to do in each training session. In order for this training programme to run smoothly, it is helpful to have a maintenance programme, much like a building or a car does, to keep all the important aspects of your everyday training in check. One of the riders I worked with in preparation for a recent Olympic Games had a new baby arrive just at the start of the Olympic year. The baby's arrival disrupted the sleep patterns of everyone in the house. Because the rider had a maintenance programme in place I noticed when the maintenance programme's 'warning light' for sleep came on and I was able to raise this with him. Without the maintenance programme the rider would not have noticed that the irregular sleep disruption was frequent enough to be an issue. Once highlighted, the rider was able to change arrangements with his partner in order that he could get the regular quality of sleep he needed.

Instigating a maintenance programme is very easy. Start by listing the items that will make up your maintenance programme. The items on this list should be general, but important, aspects of your overall training process. They are those aspects of your day-to-day life that underpin your ability to train or perform effectively and without which your ability to achieve your goals may be compromised. Your maintenance programme should be particular to you and the goals you have set. Some items may relate directly to your training programme, while others may be supplememtary to it.

Example maintenance programme items are listed in Table 6 and can include on-the-bike general and specific aspects of your training that you want to monitor closely, as well as off-the-bike training or general lifestyle items. For your maintenance programme choose or identify those things that you feel you need to monitor regularly. Then make a copy of your maintenance programme as a simple tick-list with several columns, and use one column to record the outcome for one week. In this way you can record the outcome for several weeks on a single sheet, enabling you to see at a glance if a pattern builds up over consecutive weeks. If

TABLE 6 A SAMPLE MAINTENANCE PROGRAMME

Example Maintenance Programme Items	Item
General Training	Mental skills, Strength and Conditioning, Stretching, Core Fitness
Specific Training	Sprinting, Climbing, Descending, Endurance, Off-road Skills
Lifestyle	Stress, Sleep, Nutrition, Weight

you complete the item or it goes well, give it a tick. If you do not complete an item by the end of the week or if it has not gone well put a cross against it.

Stick your maintenance programme on your fridge or somewhere similar that you visit often. This will mean your maintenance programme will be easy to monitor and update, and will serve as a source of motivation. Once your whole maintenance programme is complete for a week, maybe you can reward yourself with something from inside the fridge!

For a more advanced approach, use a spreadsheet to create and monitor your maintenance programme. Then you can easily set up a traffic light style maintenance programme dashboard. This has the added benefit of being able to highlight any patterns that emerge over several weeks. To do this instead of using ticks and crosses, colour a cell green for completed or good, red for bad or not completed, and amber if neither good nor bad applies. You will easily be able to spot where patterns appear to be developing over more than one week. Figure 14 shows an example maintenance programme from a rider I have worked with.

Maintenance Dashboard	Week 1	Week 2	Week 3	Week 4	Week 5	Week 6
Endurance						
Strength and Power						
Speed						
Skill						
Core Work						
MTB toughness						
Health						
Nutrition						
General Stress						
Sleep						
Recovery						

Fig. 14 Maintenance dashboard.

CHAPTER ELEVEN

FURTHER THOUGHTS ON TRAINING WITH POWER METERS

TURNING YOUR DREAMS INTO GOALS

Throughout this book I have emphasized the benefit of using your power meter to work towards goals if you are performance oriented. In particular I noted that it is important to be able to differentiate between your dreams and your goals. Previously, in Chapter 3, I gave examples of riders' dreams that I have regularly encountered and that frequently get confused for goals.

Dream 1: Improving your health and fitness
How attractive the new slimmer, fitter you will be after training.

Dream 2: Taking on a challenging event
Soaring up the last climb to complete a mountainous sportive just like the winner in the Tour de France.

Dream 3: Competing
Winning a race by edging out a rival on the line, or reaching a particular level of recognition or status in cycling.

These are all dreams because in their current form they are not consistent with effective goal setting. They do not provide clear, incremental and measurable objectives with a specific time frame. Whilst these examples are dreams in their current form, it is possible to turn them into goals that link to your training with a power meter. The key to doing this is that you state them as goals over which you have control, set them as incremental training goals to a deadline and, where necessary, break long-term goals into several short-term ones. Helpfully, setting goals based on training with your power meter can be very effective. In doing this you have to identify which aspects of your dreams you can control and then you can set about determining the outcome for these.

The simple rule of setting incremental training goals to a deadline holds the key to finding the goals contained within these dreams. Rather than focus on the dream outcome, think instead about the training required. You can control the training you complete in order to have a realistic chance of achieving your dream. By shifting the focus of your goal from the outcome to your training, you are no longer allowing success to be determined by how other people behave or perform. Your goal has become about you completing the training you need to succeed.

Naturally, you cannot always know how fit you will need to be or how much training you need to complete. Instead, you may have to state the level of training and fitness that you think sufficient and with which you will be satisfied. In a competition you will of course only find out at the event whether your estimate for this was correct. Ultimately there is no way around this; it is the nature of competition. It is also what makes goal setting challenging. But in focusing on your own preparation, rather than the race result, you have recast your dream as a goal you can control. Furthermore, the goals you have now established lend themselves to training with a power meter.

The outcomes for Dreams 1 and 2 can lie largely under your control and can easily be made more training focused. In Dream 1 you can reasonably expect to determine whether you lose weight and get fitter. The same is true of Dream 2, where completing a challenging sportive could depend on you developing sufficient fitness to meet the challenge.

The examples in Dream 3 are problematic, though. Winning a race, beating a rival and achieving a particular status or level of recognition are all outcomes over which you have no direct control. You cannot control the level of fitness of your competitors and therefore you cannot control the level of performance that will be required for you to win. Similarly, status and recognition typically depend on other people's perceptions of you. Again this is something you cannot control. (Actually there's an element of this in Dream 1 that I have not mentioned but I'll leave it for you to spot). So you will need to develop an alternative strategy for Dream 3.

The challenge in Dream 3 is typical of those facing a lot of riders but the approach

to dealing with it is as I have outlined above. You are goal setting to provide focus and motivation in your own personal training. However, the outcome of the race depends on how others perform and sometimes a random piece of luck. To turn Dream 3 into a goal, think about how you are going to win the race and focus on building that strength. Perhaps you decide you will edge out your rival by using your sprint. Now you can set yourself the goal of completing a particular training sprint within a target time or, better still, power output. When you reach your target sprint performance in training you will know that you are in form and ready to compete.

Finally, for these goals to follow the goal setting rule more tightly they should have a deadline and if possible an increment or improvement specified. In order to change Dream 1 to an effective goal you just need to specify exactly how much weight you plan to lose and the date by which you intend to do it. For example, a goal of losing 0.5kg per week for six weeks is much more focused. You can do the same thing for any changes in fitness you want to achieve, for example by specifying how many more watts you want to be able to sustain by a particular date in the future. Notice how these specified time-based goals present you with the opportunity to check your progress against the end goal and see if you are on track.

A simple approach for creating a goal for Dream 2 would be to have a target training session before the event. The target session could be two or three weeks before the sportive and share some of the same characteristics. These may be the same distance, time or amount of climbing, or a target average power output. Ultimately, the goal you set should be relevant to the sportive itself and give you something very focused to work towards in your training.

For Dream 3 you simply need to set yourself a deadline for when you plan to achieve your sprint goal. Note that there is another approach that can be taken with this type of event which is to set as your goal the completion of particular training sessions, rather than the level of performance in them.

For the really motivated it is possible to make your goal setting even more sophisticated. You can use your power meter to calculate the level of fitness you need in order to reach your goal. In Dream 2 you could create a project to determine exactly the power output you need in order to ride the final climb like a Tour de France winner. Working like this can give an added bite to every single training session. This really is advanced training with your power meter. It's how the British Cycling Olympic team work.

PACING

Whilst your power meter may be able to offer little advantage in coping with mental fatigue during a time trial, pacing your effort is an area in which it can really help you. Under perfect time-trial conditions on a flat course with no wind, your best time-trial race strategy is very simple: you find the highest power output that you can manage and hold this without variation for the whole race. However, the best strategy becomes a little less obvious when the time-trial conditions are not perfect. These race 'imperfections' can be caused by hills or wind. The reason that the best pacing strategy changes in less-than-perfect conditions is because the course now has slower

(uphill or headwind) and faster (downhill or tailwind) sections.

I have performed several studies that show mathematically and with power meters on a time-trial course that it is faster to vary your effort in these conditions. The ideal strategy is one where you work harder when you are racing on the slow sections of the course. On the faster sections of the course you can then afford to compensate by easing up slightly. Ultimately, you are trying to maintain a constant speed not power output, although in practice this is not usually possible. The reason that this is not usually possible is that the required variation in power output to maintain a constant speed is too great. With a power meter, however, it is possible to decide in advance what variation in power output is feasible. You can then set yourself target power outputs for the different parts of the course and monitor these with your power meter as you race.

Working with Dr Patrick Cangley, I conducted a study using power meters in exactly this way during an undulating 4km road time trial. The twenty riders in the study were asked to ride the time-trial course twice. On one occasion they rode with a constant power output of 255W, and for the alternative time trial they varied the power output in order to ride harder on the uphill sections and easier on the descents. Overall the power output for the two trials was the same. For the constant power output trial the riders averaged 411 seconds. However, in the variable power output trial their time was faster by twelve seconds. This study demonstrated that a variable power output time-trial strategy is significantly faster, even over 4km. It also showed that riders could use their power meters to help them adopt a superior variable power output pacing strategy.

So on hilly or windy courses your best strategy is to identify the slower sections of the route and try to hold an above-average power output for these sections. With a little experience and experimentation you should soon work out how much you can afford to vary your power output. In doing this you are ensuring that your power meter contributes directly to helping you achieve a faster overall time.

TRAINING RESPONDERS AND NON-RESPONDERS

Recent research has established that training at the same relative intensity affects us all differently. This can have important implications for what you should expect to accomplish and how you compare yourself to your training partners. Our recent research has shown that two riders can have a two-fold difference in how long they can train at the same relative intensity. Your TIBs have been designed to take this into account but we don't yet fully understand why this happens. Importantly, training seems to increase this variability in how long different people can keep going. After a period of training, some people will have increased their ability to keep going markedly. Others, though, may show very little improvement at all. This all seems to be part of the normal variability between riders.

Interestingly, the research on training variability doesn't stop there. Some scientists have looked at the size of your response to training. In an important study about twenty years ago, researchers gave a group of almost 500 people the same training programme to complete. The researchers found that training responses varied enormously. In fact the variation was so great that the researchers classified their participants as either training 'responders' or 'non-responders'. After ten weeks of training, fitness increased by 19 per cent on average. However, some people proved to be high responders, improving by more than 40 per cent, whilst others showed little or no change at all. One of the things that this research has found is that there appears to be a weak genetic link involved in determining whether you are a training responder or not.

What we do not know is whether changing your training can activate different genes and enable you to progress more effectively. These are very early days in this regard but there are some signs to suggest that this may be the case. The important aspect of these findings on the influence of genetics is that experimenting with your training can help you find the key to its success. If you make obvious progress with your training then it is likely that you respond well. This is where training with a power meter really pays off. You will be able to see from the data flowing from your device whether you are progressing. But if you do not see that you are getting the return from your training that others do, what then?

Finnish sports scientists have compared the responses of an endurance-cycling training programme with those for a strength training programme. Their participants had to complete both types of training to complete the study. Unsurprisingly, the scientists found that two weeks of endurance training resulted in the greatest improvement in aerobic fitness (8 per cent). Similarly, the strength training programme led to more pronounced gains in leg strength. What was particularly notable, however, was that those people whose aerobic fitness responded poorly to cycle training showed a significant improvement when they switched to strength training.

The findings of this study do not mean that you should do strength training instead of aerobic endurance training. Rather I suggest that you experiment with radically different types of training if you cannot find evidence of obvious improvement in your power meter data. Specifically, I suggest that you try including regular TIB7 high-intensity interval training sessions. The exact format of these you can vary but an example session could consist of 10 × 30-second sprints with three minutes' recovery. These sprints should be in TIB7 but paced so that you can complete the full set of 10.

The one benefit of having lots of power meter data showing you have not responded positively is that it should be easy to spot when you do!

TRADITIONAL VERSUS BLOCK TRAINING PERIODIZATION

The way that you structure or organize your training can influence its effectiveness. The concept of deliberately varying your training and its elements over time is called 'periodization'. Proponents of periodization suggest it helps provide a useful way to structure and focus your periods of training. It also encourages appropriate rest, recovery and adaptation by necessitating periods of lighter or lower-volume training too.

Periodized training was pioneered by Russian and eastern European coaches and is regarded as a traditional approach to structuring your training. More recently riders and coaches have started to structure their training in short intensive 'blocks' rather than use a longer, more traditional periodization approach. This change has been driven partly by the increased specialization of cyclists and by the desire of riders and their teams to focus on performing in specific events. This focus means that contemporary elite riders are now more flexible but focused in the way that they prepare for competitions.

There has been a little research comparing the different ways that training is structured. The findings suggest that the more contemporary approach of short block periodization training yields better training improvements than the longer traditional one.

Traditional periodization

The traditional periodization approach required coaches to think about a structure for a whole year or season. This was then broken down progressively into increasingly smaller training chunks. The largest of these training chunks is a mesocycle, which in turn can be split into intermediate macrocycles and smaller microcycles. By breaking training into cycles you control and dictate your development in a progressive and wave-like form. Each cycle contains progression to ensure your training continues to provide an appropriate overload as your fitness increases. A wave-like form is commonly adopted to ensure rest and recovery periods after hard training. For aerobic or endurance athletes a foundation of endurance training is emphasized, particularly at the start of the mesocycle (the season or year-long period). Slowly over the course of the mesocycle training volume and then intensity is increased. Finally, as you approach the peak of your season, you introduce a very specific competition phase where event-specific drills and conditioning predominate.

Whilst structuring training and co-ordinating the focus of different periods or phases is undoubtedly a positive aspect of this traditional periodization approach, there are also some limitations. The whole approach is slow, inflexible and unwieldy. If you have two events to prepare for, periodization dictates that you go back to the start again for the second. Training can become quite monotonous as the periodized structure seeks slow incremental rather than radical or marked changes.

Block periodization

Recently coaches and riders have started adopting different ways of structuring or periodizing their training. This has come about for a variety of reasons. The top teams invest heavily in winning the best races. Therefore they encourage their riders to specialize to win designated races. To do this riders and their coaches have devised more focused and concentrated ways of periodizing or chunking up their training. Typically they have a period or a block of training, followed by a block of races, and then rotate back to training again. With this kind of mixed preparation, a traditional periodization paradigm is no longer possible. Instead, each training block is specialized in nature, a highly concentrated training focus maintained with very limited aspects of fitness being developed. The planning process revolves around sequencing these specialized blocks. Your overall performance is enhanced by the superimposition of fitness from one block to the next.

Throughout this book I have outlined training in terms of block periodization rather than a more traditional approach. To adopt block periodization for your own training, the basic principles are as follows. Identify the different training blocks you will need to include in your training programme and their training sequence. You can return to a training block more than once but do not position two identical blocks consecutively. Ensure that you have a high concentration of training workloads within a block. To achieve this keep your training blocks short. The exact length of time for one block may vary but they typically last up to fourteen days rather than several weeks. At the end of the block you should include a recovery period with an emphasis on light TIB1 riding before starting the next block. Within a training block, target a minimal number of fitness aspects. Make your training in a specific TIB the key feature of that block. Plan your consecutive blocks to build your overall fitness as part of your overall training strategy and programme. If your event requires good endurance, aerobic fitness and climbing, you will need to make each of these the focus of different training blocks.

THRESHOLD AND POLARIZED TRAINING

Polarizing your training refers to the way in which your training is distributed across different TIBs. Most endurance riders appear to follow one of two distinctly different models of distributing their training. These have been called polarized- and threshold-type training. Which model riders use may

Michael Kwiatkawski during the thirteenth mountain stage of the 2014 Tour de France. (Pierre-Jean Durieu/Shutterstock.com)

be the result of deliberate planning for some, whilst for others it may simply reflect what feels right or habitual patterns of training that have been adopted without specific planning.

The threshold model of training distribution is one where most of your training is accomplished at a moderate intensity (in other words in TIB2, TIB3 and TIB4). In particular, very little training time is spent at intensities above TIB4. It is a classic or traditional endurance training approach and tends not to feature much high-intensity interval training. In contrast, in polarized training more training time is spent at a moderate intensity of TIB2. However, unlike the threshold model the remaining training time is focused at the high intensities of TIB5, TIB6 and TIB7.

You can examine the distribution of your training across different TIBs by looking at the percentage of your total training time that you spend in each TIB. For example, if out of ten hours of training in one week you spend eight in TIB1 and TIB2, your distribution is 80 per cent. Similarly, if you spend the remaining two hours training in TIB5 and TIB6 this is 20 per cent. This would be an example of an 80:20 polarized training model. (Notice that there is a gap in the middle that constitutes TIB3 and TIB4 training.) A threshold distribution of training does not have this clear differentiation between moderate and high-intensity training, and it cannot be polarized in this way as you will spend the majority of time in TIB2, TIB3 and TIB4, with very little above this.

Anecdotally, the 80:20 ratio of low-intensity training to high-intensity training seems to be employed by many successful athletes. Scientifically it is not yet possible to explain why this should be more effective than a threshold model. Part of the benefit of a polarized model of training may be the amount of recovery time that it permits; you are capable of sustaining a training programme with regular and challenging bouts of high-intensity training only if contrasted with a reasonable volume of low-intensity training. Increasing the intensity of the overall programme has been shown to be associated with symptoms of overtraining and burnout.

To date not many studies into this have been completed. Two recent studies, however, both show that polarized training resulted in greater training improvements than a threshold approach. My own research on elite riders' power meter data suggests they adopt a sort of polarized training model to cope with higher-intensity training and racing. The findings are shown in Figure 15 which depicts how time spent in different TIBs changed from before to during the competitive season. The power meter data were compared for the riders' training in January/February and May/June. From the changes in training you can see that the riders' training has become increasingly polarized. Time spent training in the extreme intensities of TIB1, TIB5 and TIB6 has increased, whilst time in the middle intensities of TIB2, TIB3 and TIB4 has reduced. (Note TIB6 and TIB7 have been combined on this plot.)

These shifts in how training time was spent suggest that the riders have polarized their training. In order to increase the amount of TIB6 training they complete, they also have to spend more time recovering at TIB1 between intervals. In addition, because the intensity of their training has increased they are spending less time in TIB2 and TIB3. Interestingly, these observations also suggest that the riders are not following a traditional periodization approach. If they were you would expect to see some progression in TIB2, TIB3 and TIB4 rather than the opposite.

I should add that I do not think these findings should be interpreted to mean that threshold training or TIB2, TIB3 and TIB4 are not effective. I believe they still have an important role in your overall training programme. Rather, when you are looking to find those last little incremental gains in your fitness, then you should consider adding higher-intensity training rather than more TIB2 to TIB4 training.

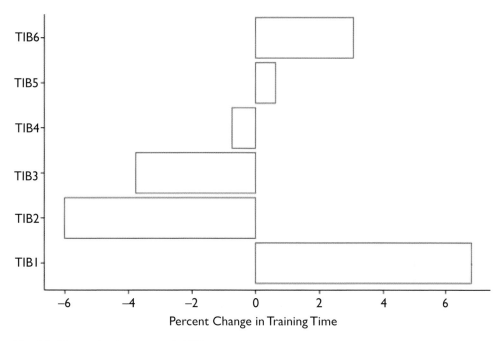

Fig. 15 Change in time spent in TIB.

APPENDIX 1: EXAMPLE WORKOUTS

RECOVERY RIDE – TIB1

This is an easy recovery ride. Ride comfortably, spinning a low gear. You should keep your heart rate and power output low throughout. Keep the ride to less than ninety minutes otherwise it will become more than just a recovery, even when ridden at TIB1. This is a good ride to do with a friend or to a cafe.

LONG ENDURANCE RIDE – TIB1

This is an easy endurance ride. Ride steadily, keeping up a brisk cadence. You can allow your power to vary with the terrain as it will inevitably increase beyond TIB1 at times. But use your power meter to make sure you ease back on long climbs and ride close to or within TIB1. This type of ride is primarily used in training for very long events or if you are building up your fitness from a low base, therefore it would usually be for two hours or more. Try and move your training into TIB2 once your fitness allows it. This is another good ride to do with a companion.

MEDIUM ENDURANCE RIDE – TIB2

This is a core ride to develop endurance and aerobic fitness. Keep a very steady consistent effort at TIB2 for 1.5 to 3 hours. This type of training provides the cornerstone conditioning for an endurance rider. On a steady endurance ride like this you should find you always have to make a bit of an effort to maintain your target power output but without feeling stressed. Try to produce the necessary power output by keeping your cadence high rather than by pressing harder on the pedals or churning a big gear. Your recovery from shorter rides can be quite fast and back-to-back sessions should be possible if you are reasonably fit. When you are preparing for an important event you can consider doing this kind of ride as part of a split day, with a more intense session later. For longer rides make sure you take a couple of bottles of water with you and that you drink them.

LONG MODERATE ENDURANCE RIDE – TIB2

This is a serious ride for building endurance. Riding at TIB2 for more than three hours can become quite challenging. For these rides you should take something with you to eat and drink. Unless you are very fit you can expect to take more than twenty-four hours to recover from a long TIB2 ride. These rides are impractical to do in a large group because you will slide back into TIB1 when you are not on the front, but they can work well with just one or two training partners if you are all trying to complete a similar session. If you are doing long rides such as these then you are trying to really develop your endurance. Make sure you eat and drink properly so that you can maintain your target power output even at the end of the ride; riding slowly because you have slipped up with your nutrition is not an effective way to become a faster rider. However, you can increase the endurance demands of your long rides by training first thing in the morning without breakfast. In this situation wait until you are a few minutes into your ride before you start eating and drinking normally.

MEDIUM HARD ENDURANCE RIDE – TIB3

This is a hard ride done to build endurance and aerobic fitness. Along with TIB2 rides, brisk TIB3 rides form one of the most typical sessions for an endurance rider. During these rides you will normally need to keep a regular eye on your power meter to ensure you are maintaining the necessary power output. On descents and in tailwinds it may not be possible to produce sufficient power to stay within your TIB. In these situations it can be helpful to use your power meter to display your average power output during your ride. As with TIB2 your recovery from short rides can be quite fast, but longer rides can quickly become very demanding and delay your recovery notably.

LONG VERY DEMANDING ENDURANCE RIDE – TIB2 AND TIB3

This is a very challenging endurance ride. If you are already very fit you may consider mixing TIB2 and TIB3 in the same training session on a long ride of over two hours. This type of training is useful for preparing for long road races and very hilly events as the stress is quite similar. You can alternate ten- to thirty-minute blocks of TIB2 and TIB3, depending on your goals and current level of fitness. For really challenging sessions, perhaps just before your main event, 'back load' your TIB3 intervals. Back loading involves waiting to introduce the demanding TIB3 intervals until you are in the later stages of a long training ride. Back loading intervals will really test and develop your endurance fitness.

RACE-PACE EFFORTS – TIB4

Often referred to as threshold training, this type of training familiarizes your body with the stress of competing or exploring your limits. This kind of training can be done as a controlled consistent effort or broken down into long intervals lasting five to ten minutes. You will learn pace control and to concentrate on producing a hard, sustained effort. Use your power meter when riding to help you learn how to judge these kind of efforts. Introduced into a long ride, TIB4 efforts will make the ride very demanding and you will probably need to ride easily between efforts. However, hilly rides often take this form with TIB4 climbs interspersed with easier riding and descending in between.

LONG HIGH-INTENSITY INTERVALS – TIB5 AND TIB6

There are many ways interval training can be divided up. Experiment with different permutations to create novelty in your programme. Less commonly used interval structures include pyramid and Bondarenko sessions where the intervals and the pace vary within the same session. Typically with these kinds of interval sessions you are looking for ways to impose a race pace (or above) type of stress on your body. The aim is to accustom you to coping with the kind fatigue that these high-intensity efforts promote. Normally recovery for this type of session is partial or incomplete between efforts. To progress this kind of interval training you can reduce your recovery, as well as making the intervals longer or more intense.

SHORT HIGH-INTENSITY INTERVALS – TIB5, TIB6 AND TIB7

These interval sessions are normally focused on developing your top-end power output. By keeping the efforts reasonably short you are able to ensure that you repeatedly develop very high power outputs. Typically these intervals may be performed as individual efforts or short sets of two to five sprints before a longer recovery. As the aim is to ensure you develop a very high power output, you allow yourself a good recovery period between efforts or sets. This is in contrast to the longer intervals. End the session when you are no longer capable of hitting your target power output. A less common short-interval structure is to use repeated six-second efforts with twenty-four seconds recovery. Due to the short sprint you make each time, it is possible to repeat these intervals continuously for ten to twenty minutes. This type of session is very different from most other types of interval training. It is ideal for MTB riders who have to vary their power output markedly when off-road.

APPENDIX 2: EXAMPLE TRAINING BLOCKS

ROAD RACER SEVEN-DAY BLOCK

Road Racer 7 Day Block **Example Training Programme A**	Intensity	**Duration (minutes)**
Day 1	TIB2	120
Day 2	TIB4	25
Day 3	TIB1	60
Day 4	TIB2 and TIB7	60
Day 5	TIB1	60
Day 6	TIB4	30
Day 7	No Training	
Total minutes		355

Road Racer 7 Day Block **Example Training Programme B**	Intensity	**Duration (minutes)**
Day 1	TIB2	150
Day 2	TIB1	45
Day 3	TIB4	20
Day 4	TIB1	60
Day 5	TIB2	90
Day 6	TIB4 and TIB7	35
Day 7	No Training	
Total minutes		400

Road Racer 7 Day Block Example Training Programme C	Intensity	Duration (minutes)
Day 1	TIB5	20
Day 2	TIB1	90
Day 3	TIB4 and TIB7	30
Day 4	TIB1	60
Day 5	TIB2	90
Day 6	TIB2 and TIB3	180
Day 7	No Training	
Total minutes		470

TT RIDER SEVEN-DAY BLOCK

TT Rider 7 Day Block Example Training Programme A	Intensity	Duration (minutes)
Day 1	TIB4	30
Day 2	TIB1	60
Day 3	TIB5 and TIB7	30
Day 4	TIB1	60
Day 5	TIB2	90
Day 6	TIB2 and TIB3	120
Day 7	Day off	
Total minutes		390

SPORTIVE RIDER
SEVEN-DAY BLOCK

Sportive Rider 7 Day Block **Example Training Programme A**	Intensity	**Duration (minutes)**
Day 1	TIB2	90
Day 2	TIB1	60
Day 3	TIB4	20
Day 4	TIB1	60
Day 5	TIB2	60
Day 6	TIB5 and TIB7	20
Day 7	No Training	
Total minutes		310

Sportive Rider 7 Day Block **Example Training Programme B**	Intensity	**Duration (minutes)**
Day 1	TIB2	60
Day 2	TIB4	30
Day 3	TIB1	60
Day 4	TIB2	120
Day 5	TIB1	60
Day 6	TIB2 and TIB4	90
Day 7	No Training	
Total minutes		420

Sportive Rider 7 Day Block **Example Training Programme C**	Intensity	**Duration (minutes)**
Day 1	TIB4	25
Day 2	TIB1	45
Day 3	TIB2	90
Day 4	TIB1	45
Day 5	TIB7	20
Day 6	TIB2 and TIB3	120
Day 7	No Training	
Total minutes		345

TRIATHLETE SEVEN-DAY BLOCK

Triathlete 7 Day Block **Example Training Programme A**	Intensity	**Duration (minutes)**
Day 1	Run	
Day 2	TIB4 or TIB6	25
Day 3	Swim	
Day 4	TIB1	60
Day 5	Run	
Day 6	TIB2	90
Day 7		
Total Cycling minutes		175

Triathlete 7 Day Block **Example Training Programme B**	Intensity	**Duration (minutes)**
Day 1	Run	
Day 2	TIB5	30
Day 3	Swim	
Day 4	TIB1	90
Day 5	Run	
Day 6	TIB2 and TIB3	120
Day 7		
Total Cycling minutes		240

MTB RIDER SEVEN-DAY BLOCK

MTB Rider 7 Day Block Example Training Programme A	Intensity	Duration (minutes)
Day 1	TIB2	90
Day 2	TIB4 and TIB7	25
Day 3	TIB1	60
Day 4	Off-Road ride	90
Day 5	No Training	0
Day 6	TIB2 and TIB3	90
Day 7	TIB1	45
Total minutes		400

MTB Rider 7 Day Block Example Training Programme B	Intensity	Duration (minutes)
Day 1	TIB2	90
Day 2	Off-Road ride	90
Day 3	TIB1	60
Day 4	TIB2 and TIB5	90
Day 5	TIB1	0
Day 6	TIB6	30
Day 7	No Training	
Total minutes		360

INDEX

muscle or muscular 47, 55, 69–70, 101, 103, 105, 107

O

Obree, Graeme 11

P

pace or pacing 11, 14, 27, 63–4, 67, 69, 79, 84, 88, 94, 100, 107, 111, 115–16, 125–6, 127, 134
peak power (see power output)
peak 31, 90, 116, 128
planning training 13–14, 16, 23, 30, 31–45, 55, 57, 93, 111, 116, 118, 128–9
power output
average 42–3, 77, 82–7, 90–1, 95–7, 99, 101, 111–12, 116, 118–19, 124, 126, 133
normalized 95
peak 26, 69, 102–6, 115

R

races and racing
MTB 66, 89, 112–15, 135
road 9–11, 64, 67, 69, 71, 88, 90, 91, 96–107, 112, 133, Appendix 2
time-trial 11, 64, 66–7, 70, 71, 79, 88, 90–1, 98–9, 103, 106, 107–10, 125
triathlon 23, 55, 71, 88, 90, 115–16
rating of perceived exertion (see RPE)
recovery 14, 39, 46, 47–53, 57–8, 61–2, 64, 67–70, 80, 91–3, 95, 106, 109–10, 112–13, 115–16, 127–8, 130, 132–4
road races (see races)
RPE 61–2, 64–5, 119–21
rules (for training) 34, 53, 56, 89, 123–4

S

scientist 9, 10, 28, 42, 49–50, 53, 55, 57, 64–5, 70, 77, 93, 103, 105, 107, 126
software 11, 26–9, 42, 85, 95, 117–18, 121

speed (see training)
sprinting 38, 69, 71, 97, 101–7
stage race 10, 50, 62

T

temperature 10, 21, 52, 105
tempo 63, 112, 118
testing with your power meter 12, 22, 72–6, 82–6, 105, 107, 120
threshold 61, 64–5, 67, 128–30, 134
time trials (see races)
training
duration 61, 63, 78, 80, 83, 91, 116
frequency 53, 78, 80, 90–1, 116
intensity 12, 14, 21–2, 39, 42, 47, 57–70, 76, 78–80, 82–6, 93–5
intensity bands (TIBs) 14, 39, 42, 47, 57–70, 81–6
intervals 35, 54, 67, 70, 93–4, 127, 129, 134
load 42, 80–1, 116
speed 14, 21–3, 27, 42, 61–3, 74, 87, 96, 101, 103, 108, 110–12, 119, 125
variation 21, 26, 56, 87, 91, 113–14, 117, 119, 125–6
volume 61, 80–1, 116, 127
triathlon (see races)
triathlete 9, 54, 115–18, Appendix 2

V

variation (see training)
VO$_2$max (see aerobic capacity)

W

warm up 69, 84, 103, 105, 115, 120
watt 19, 26–7, 60–1, 67, 84, 117–18, 124
work rate 17–30, 49–50, 52, 62–4, 70–1, 76–7, 88, 94, 114
world record 10, 11

Z

zone 57–8, 67

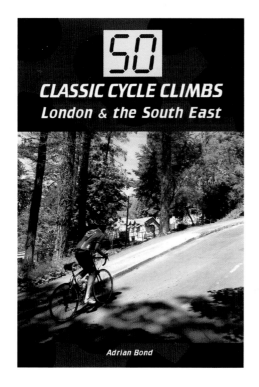

50 CLASSIC CYCLE CLIMBS
London & the South East

Adrian Bond

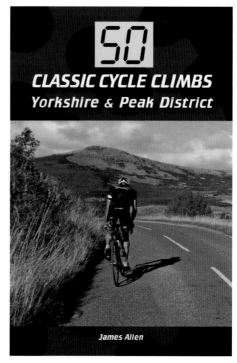

50 CLASSIC CYCLE CLIMBS
Yorkshire & Peak District

James Allen

FOREWORD BY
DARREN SMITH AND JODIE STIMPSON

100 ESSENTIAL TRIATHLON SESSIONS

STEVE TREW AND
DAN BULLOCK

THE DEFINITIVE TRAINING PROGRAMME FOR ALL SERIOUS TRIATHLETES

CYCLE
ROAD RACING

TOM NEWMAN